Facing Hate: Mem

MW01656772

Mr. Jeub teaching online from his home office.

Chris Jeub is creator of popular curriculum and resources for academic speakers and debaters. An English teacher by trade, Chris manages an online database for speech and debate competitors while teaching 7th grade language arts at a local charter school. Most of all Mr. Jeub loves hanging out at home with his wife, Wendy, and his kids — more than half of whom are adults — and especially the grandchildren that keep growing in number.

Current count: 16 children and 12 grandchildren. The year of this book's release, Chris and Wendy are celebrating 30 years of marriage.

FACING HATE

Memoir of a Social Smear

Chris Jeub

Published in the United States by Monument Ridge Publishing, an imprint of Monument Ridge Publishing Group, a division of Monument Ridge Ltd. of Monument, Colorado.

All photos courtesy of the author. Names and identifying characteristics have been changed or withheld to protect privacy.

ISBN 9798587711211

Printed in the United States of America

For everyone who bears the rare name of Jeub, especially my children and grandchildren.

And for anyone whose name has been smeared. May they find this memoir helpful as they find the courage to face those who hate them, recover any lost relationships they suffered, and reclaim their personal reputations.

Contents

Prologue

I remained largely silent following my social smear. It started in 2014, and its details you will soon learn. Several years passed. Slowly. Sometimes agonizingly. And I finally had to speak.

Since coming forward to address my personal drama, I have received letters from people who suffered similar public shaming, humiliation for whatever perceived offense, attack from online strangers (to whom I will refer in this book as "the mob"), and more. Before I tell you about mine, I will share with you theirs.

> *I'm newly married living in a rural area with my wife and newborn son. I work construction during the day, but on the weekends I like to ride my off-road motorcycle in the ditches of the country. I love the country life! I appreciate my next-door neighbor, too, or at least I used to. He had been complaining to the other neighbors of my loud motorcycle and has posted derogatory insults online about me. I live next door, and he has never once mentioned having a problem with the cycle, but he feels fine posting his complaints about me online.*
>
> *—A Neighbor*

> *Both my husband and I married after divorce, most of our children adults, and have made the best of our blended family. I have gotten along with most of his children and their spouses fine, but one of my husband's sons insists on seeing the worst in everything I do or say. He obviously doesn't appreciate*

me, but he doesn't keep his opinions to himself. He puts me down at family gatherings and gossips about me behind my back. Most of the other kids have joined him. Recently they have unfriended me or blocked me from their Facebook accounts. Yesterday I was uninvited from a baby shower. My nickname, I heard, has become "wicked stepmother." I honestly have not one wicked thought in my mind for any of my husband's children.

—A Stepmother

I have to admit, I did lose my cool with this student. He was hijacking my middle school science class with outbursts and immature fart noises. I barked at him to be quiet several times, eventually threatening to send him to the principal's office. We talked privately after class. When he isn't trying to impress his friends he receives correction much better, and we had a fairly good conversation ending on the hope that he would behave better the next day. I was shocked to read a Facebook flair-up that evening on our school's parents page. The mom posted mostly everything of the uncomfortable classroom situation, minus her son's fart noises or the constructive conversation we had after class. Other parents piled on accusing me of being impatient, unprofessional, a bad teacher. My phone rang as I was reading the posts. It was my principal. I am to meet with my administrators tomorrow morning.

—A Teacher

I love my son. He's in his twenties now and living with his male partner. I had raised him in a conservative home advocating marriage between a man and woman only, but he obviously rejected that idea. I would like to be able to understand him and his life choices, but he hasn't ever allowed me the opportunity. Instead, my son has gone public with a narrative of being ostracized by his parents, being "kicked out" of the home when he came out as gay. Nothing remotely close to this is true. Today my son and partner adopted a child and I am forbidden to attend any family events. On Facebook he references me as a gay-bashing bigot, but I have never participated in anything of the sort.

—A Dad

The dress could not be adjusted any more. This bride was pregnant and the wedding was drawing near, so I gently made the only recommendation that made sense: she should buy a new wedding dress and start over. The bride-to-be appeared to take the bad news in stride, accepted her full refund that I offered and went to find a new dress that would serve her on her wedding day. I was shocked, then, to see a blistering 1-star review on our Google page about how my small sewing business ruined her wedding. She left out the truth of her pregnancy and her full refund, and added untrue accusations of me being impatient and rude. My business relies on reviews; everyone reads them before hiring a seamstress. And online reviews last forever!

—A Business Owner

Do any of these ring true for you? Prior to my own social smearing, I likely would not have identified at all. But I now connect with each of them in a personal way. They trigger deep, depressing similarities to my story that have left me figuratively beaten down. It is difficult to understand without walking through it yourself. I do not wish the experience on anyone, but it's an experience fewer and fewer of us are successfully escaping today.

"Social smearing" is the use of electronic media to tear down and destroy (or at least attempt to destroy) an individual or business. In recent years this powerful tool has become the weapon of choice for disgruntled employees, estranged relatives, disturbed neighbors, and any rebel-with-a-cause with a cell phone and internet access. Gossips have always been with us, but large-scale, wide-reaching social smearing used to be reserved for movie stars and politicians, and consumption of retail-level gossip was buy-in only at the newsstand or grocery store checkout line. Not today. We all "buy in" to social smearing when we search on Google, scroll down our Facebook or Instagram feed, or check our email. And if we're buying in to the pain of others, then we're at risk of feeling that pain ourselves.

Even if we're not buying in, we're at risk.

You and I have shrugged our shoulders and not given much thought to the social smear of a distant friend or casual acquaintance. But when you see your own name broadcast across the internet coupled with fabricated (or at least exaggerated and twisted) stories of your personal life, your heart couldn't sink lower and your head couldn't spin faster. Some of us have lashed out in anger. Others have hidden away. None of us has overcome the lasting damage social smears do to our self-esteem or reputation. Whatever the degree of social smearing we have been subjected to — and no matter how fair or unfair the smears have been — all of us come away weathered, tarnished, shamed.

This is the new world in which we live.

But there are glimmers of hope amid the harassment. Social smearing *can* be overcome with principled, strategic actions that can, in fact, make you a better person with a stronger personal — and even *online* – narrative than you had before your social smear. I can't wait to get to that more wholesome part of my journey. But first I must tell my own tale of woe, the story of my smear. We will sit and talk, you and I, about the six years of dealing with the ashes of volcanic fallout. I am happy to report that I didn't lash out in anger through all of this — and you'll see why later — but I didn't hide away either. And several events followed my apparent ruined reputation that helped give me a better understanding of the entire world of social media. I discovered ways to "lean in" on the smear, listen to the hidden truths embedded within it, and adapt to the challenges that come with the unique mixture of shame and injustice that accompanies so many social smears. I even learned how to turn the tables on a smear campaign, sometimes turning once-bitter enemies into lasting friends and advocates for my renewed online reputation.

I conclude this book with pointed direction for anyone facing social smearing. It seems like this new phenomenon of social smearing brings a wide range of often useless advice from people who have no idea what it's like to be personally accused, tried and convicted without ever having their chance at rebuttal or day in court. My advice, then, is hard won, tried and true in the fires of personal circumstance. I'm confident it will help you through your trial of social smearing, whether it has already come or is merely waiting in the wings.

I've walked through the shadow of online death from beginning to end and have come out not only alive, but stronger for the experience. I'm glad to say that I am a better person — a better father, husband, businessman and teacher — than I was before. I won't submit to the untruth of the initial smear, but I will submit to you the proactive responses I eventually figured out, that have brought about a much better resolution than I could have ever dreamed.

Chris Jeub

I loved every bit of Wendy's beautiful single-parent family.

We married in 1991.

Chapter 1: The Jeub Family

The days leading up to our social smear were mixed with more joy than anguish. Married 23 years, Wendy and I were taking life in stride, embracing marriage and parenting with enthusiasm, just the way we liked it. We were transparent with many of our personal issues — writing books and publishing articles about some of them — private about others that we were uneasy about, even embarrassed. Perhaps you've read some of our stories. We used to enjoy sharing them, especially with those who identified with our joys and struggles. You didn't need to be a crazy-large family to be counted among the friends of the Jeubs. We were hospitable, open and kind to everyone who came by to visit our cozy home, now brimming with *sixteen* awesome children.

That's how our family got "famous," if you can call it that. Sixteen kids is something to visit! Sixteen little ones makes for great TV! Sixteen heirs to my dominion sounds just a little kooky, right? But I like to think people found us interesting for more than just the number of children we had. Wendy and I were, and still are, diehard romantics who loved to go on adventures together, unafraid of bringing our teaming horde along with us. We were a sight to see! Even trips to the supermarket turned the heads of most folks. I like to think our spirit was contagious and fun. This made us an attractive family to profile on television, allowed us to publish and sell books about our life, and become favored speakers to audiences of parents and educators. We had a lot to share, and we were happy to share it.

If you don't know me, my wife, or my family — or if you don't relate at all with my lots-o'-kids lifestyle — that's quite all right. This book isn't really about large families at all. It's about social smearing, a stark reality that was a sucker punch to the gut for us on October 2, 2014. We weren't hit by a random stranger online, an acquaintance at church, or even a friend. We were walloped from within, by a band of our own daughters who drummed up a narrative that irreparably hurt our reputation. We were among the first to experience a now-common phenomenon, and chances are good you picked this book up because you, likewise, have suffered at the hands of a social smear.

I wish I could start this book by assuring you that social smearing does not and cannot define you, but that would be a lie. My family's life will never fully return to the fun days of adventure and growth that we shared all those years ago. We are permanently marked with a narrative quite opposite of what was true. There are those who continue to this day to ravage us online, refusing any of our attempts to explain, thinking our talk of love and the "greatest commandment" of our family to be merely a facade, designed to hide cruelty and dysfunction.

So, by definition, the Jeubs are now a family that has suffered a social smear that nearly ruined us. That story started six years ago, but it helps to know the background leading up to our devastating day. Let me introduce you to the Jeub family, established nearly 30 years ago, when Wendy and I first met …

Wendy and I have little sisters who set us up to meet in late June, 1990. Our sisters were best friends in high school, had just graduated, and were throwing a private party for friends. Wendy and I were the older ones among the 18-year-old "kids." I asked right away about Wendy — she sure was cute, and our eyes met more than once as people gathered. "She has two kids," was what I was told. I was a child of the '80s — part of the Mötley Crüe "Girls, Girls, Girls" culture — so details of a troubled life didn't bother me. Truth be known, even in my youth I was growing tired of being single and was looking for a mate to start a family. Getting a head start was not off the table, so I asked Wendy on a date. Come with me to the fireworks on the 4th of July, I said. Her kids were away with their grandmother that week, so she said yes. I like to say to this day, "There has been fireworks ever since!"

It was perfect, nearly scripted out of a romantic movie. I picked her up, we drove to a city park, we laid out a blanket and talked for two hours, watching the sunset and awaiting the fireworks. We cuddled, enjoying the warmth of a new relationship. Wendy was incredibly interesting, and she found me the same. It's hard to believe this, but we even talked about how many children we would like to have when married "to someone, someday." I said 10. She laughed. This led to deeper discussion of her teenage pregnancies and two daughters. We enjoyed the evening because we were both considering one another's interests, as young lovers should.

Wendy was one year into a job following a business tech school degree; and I was a new transfer to the town's university, working my way toward becoming a school teacher. My parents had just moved from my graduating town, so most of my close friends were just enough distance away to free my time for this new friendship. Wendy and I spent nearly every day and evening together. One week in, Wendy's four-year-old came home. A week after that, her six-year-old. I was slowly but surely being weaned out of the wild-and-crazy single life, attracted to Wendy's beautiful single-parent family, and I loved every bit of it. We married 10 months later.

You can't easily split 23 years in half, but it's helpful when looking at our marriage up to that fateful October 2nd, in 2014. Consider the first half to be our "convicting" years, the second our "growing" years. Even though I had roughly two years of college remaining when we married, I loaded up on credit hours and finished in one, graduating *magna cum laude*. Adopting Wendy's daughters was a legally grueling process, but we managed to finish that, also within a year. Wendy quit her job when I finished college, and I worked for two years as a produce manager while picking up substitute teaching jobs in several Minnesota school districts. By the mid-'90s I landed my first English teaching job in North Dakota, just over the Minnesota border, not too far from extended family.

I call these "convicting" years because, despite conventional wisdom of the times, we kept having children. Lots of "firsts" in this time of our life. We had our first child together in 1992, barely a year into our new marriage. The next — our fourth daughter, counting Wendy's first two children — came in 1994, after which we moved into our first house on a first-year teacher's salary. Our first three sons came three years in a row: 1996, 1997 and 1998. By the time our last Minnesota child was born in 2000, I had changed my teaching jobs three times, ending with a layoff from a district-wide teacher reduction. I liked teaching, especially coaching debate, but my career as a teacher seemed to not be working for my family.

I was 30 years old, unemployed, married with eight children, licensed to be an English teacher. Funny, in my mind's eye I was still a 20-year-old Van Halen fan, having fun hurdling over every obstacle that came my way. But my life of "conviction" led me elsewhere, and if you follow your true, God-given convictions, you will be in for a much greater adventure than what popular culture offers. At the time I asked, "Who will hire a young dad of eight kids?" Focus on the Family in Colorado Springs, that's who. A couple of years prior I had connected with their teachers ministry, so I reconnected and asked for a job. My English degree landed me in editing, eventually becoming a Senior Online Editor in the brave new world of the internet. This four-and-a-half year stint wrapped up my Convicting Years.

Conviction. That word sounds negative. For me, it was very positive and rewarding. As we welcomed children into our family, both Wendy and I had strong faith that God would provide financially, emotionally and physically. We welcomed two more children right away in Colorado, officially becoming parents of 10 — double-digits! — and we held little conviction to stop. We believed (and still do) that children are blessings from God, so why not welcome more? Our personal conviction — very personal to us, not something we think everyone should hold — was to welcome more Jeub children. And our life is most bountiful because of it.

Our next decade (the second half of those first 23 years of marriage) consisted of our "growing" years. Life became more complicated, more painful, but we kept having children. Our 11th child came about the time I finished my MBA at Regis University. Wendy encouraged me all the way. But it was a mixture of joy and anguish. I was let go from Focus on the Family after an inner-office disagreement that got ugly. I had already started my masters program and I had a small-but-growing publishing business on the side, so I took a severance payment and voluntarily resigned. Then the twins came — "We skipped a dozen!" I would say — giving us a grand total of 13 children in 2005. I was 35, father to 13, a self-employed business owner, husband to a still-very-cute five-foot-one-inch blonde who I couldn't keep my hands off of!

Sounds like a TV reality show, doesn't it? Well, yes, it does. Shortly after the twins' birth, some friends suggested our names to The Learning Channel for a series of family shows. The producers wanted to film us for a week during our September Jeub Birthday Bash, our yearly birthday party for all of our children, a unique large-family tradition we created in Minnesota and still keep to this day. We agreed, and for a week in September 2006, we blew the minds of a crew of four single guys — two cameramen, a sound guy and a producer — as they captured the "reality" of the Jeub family.

Reality TV was a relatively new concept at the time, and we were lucky enough to have one of its founders be our onsite producer. The program was called *Kids by the Dozen* and featured a total of seven families, but the first and second seasons were vastly different. The first was, I believe, more genuine. All three families getting screen time in that first year, us included, got a chance to display their real-life joys and genuine struggles for the camera. The second season, in contrast, was largely staged, every episode containing a fabricated drama imagined by the new onsite producer. (The original producer who did our episode had been replaced.) I didn't like the second season nearly as much as the first. Neither did the viewers, I reckon. The show was not renewed for a third season.

Our event was the birthday bash, but our struggle dealt with the estrangement of our oldest daughter, at the time a single mom who had left our family. This was not fabricated. She left our home at 19 in a huff, had a child out of wedlock, and was hellbent on wanting nothing to do with her family. At least that's what she communicated on her way out. I'm ashamed to say this now, but we tried to hide her from the camera.

Again, heavenly conviction is a good thing, and if you follow it you will seldom be disappointed with the outcome. After keeping the door shut on this "skeleton" for the full week of filming, we felt a strong conviction to share this reality to our "reality" producer. The result? Nearly 50 hours of birthday party scenes, documentation of our family's school bus conversion, our homeschooling and my family business ended up on the editing floor. This was just too "juicy" to turn a blind camera eye to, the producer decided. Estrangement! Banishment! He returned to New York, pitched this new "angle" and then contacted our oldest daughter asking for an onscreen interview. She agreed to be filmed for "the other side" to the Jeub family story. And so it was that our private family drama ended up becoming the most significant public part of the show.

I am so very pleased I overcame the temptation to avoid my convictions, but it was risky. The TV producers could have made us look like crazy, angry parents who booted their innocent daughter out on the streets for petty reasons. I suppose some people saw us as such, but the show felt well balanced to us. It presented the achingly common conflict of an adult child pushing against the boundaries of her loving parents. The show wisely avoided the details of the separation, instead focusing on the *reality* of it, and our attempts to reconcile and make matters better. Rather than us pointing fingers at one another and creating a family feud for all the world to judge, we expressed our frustrations *and love* for our daughter, with the hope of a reconciliation that we all desired.

That's how the show ended, but not our story. We did end up bringing our oldest daughter back into the family — and our grandson, too! — even before our episode reached America's screens. This larger story is captured in our book *Love in the House*, a loose play on lyrics from a favorite TobyMac song, "Love is in the house when the house is packed." Our eldest daughter even helped us get the story straight, a story of apologies and redemption and renewal. It was a beautiful time in our family.

Our book capitalized on our television popularity at the time, which has been criticized by some as opportunistic. We see it differently. We wanted to reveal our family's journey to encourage other families — especially young couples struggling with their children — that their love and sacrifice is worth it. As I've said, follow *conviction* and you will seldom be disappointed, whether you're raising little ones with the most basic questions about the most basic needs of a child, or if you're struggling with a rebellious teenager whose troubles are deep waters of doubt and confusion.

Our 46-minute television show was a peek into our home. Our book pulled back the curtains for more.

How ironic. We don't even have curtains on most of our windows. And curtains will became a significant metaphor later when our life caves in.

You can see it clearly now. Our 23 years of family life was sprinkled with both joy and anguish. It's easy to write about the joy, and getting pats on the back for being a "perfect" family feels momentarily pleasing. Of course we're *not* perfect, and pain is where people relate to us. I have found that whenever I gather the courage to speak out about the pains of life, I help others. The *conviction* to be publicly honest leads to my most significant *growth*. That has been my life, especially now dealing with the pain of social smearing.

From when our television show released in 2007 to October 2014 — seven strong years — we leaned in on our pain. You've struggled with finances? We have, too. So we created an audio guide called *Cheaper by the Dozen* and traveled to speak at churches and homeschool conferences about how to raise multiple children on a tight budget. We eat like kings in our home, largely because of Wendy's cooking prowess, but how does she feed so many? It's a great question. So Wendy wrote two cookbooks, *Love in the Kitchen, Volumes 1* and 2. They are the best cookbooks on the market, in my humble opinion, because they're full of *real* recipes from a *real* family with *real* ingredients you can find in most homes. How about weight loss? Wendy has even written a diet book, *Love in a Diet*. For someone with 16 children who looks as awesome as she does, countless numbers of moms wanted to know her secrets.

During those years we had three more children and suffered two miscarriages. And so the mix of joy and the anguish persisted. The kid count was then (likely) capped at 16. I still had my family business (a curriculum publishing business for academic speakers and debaters), and though it had provided modestly for my family, it has also had its share of pain. The debate league I served suffered a bitter split, some of my former students organized to be openly critical of my programs, and some local coaches boycotted my publications for a while. Business flagged as a result. We were accosted a bitter church split that left us "house churching" for several years, and we have wrestled with our relationship with God in our own personal way, largely because of how painful religious legalism can be. Our relationship with our oldest again went through another family drama when we refused — as politely as we could — to include her boyfriend in our family Christmas letter. She wanted us to call him her husband, but they weren't married. And we were once again stuck in that tight rub between expediency and conviction.

These are real struggles in our family. And they aren't the only ones. I don't intentionally keep any of them from you; I just haven't shared them yet. Some are as yet unresolved, and some of them are best kept private. Close friends know more, but none know all. How could they? Wendy and I are busily hustling children to and fro, juggling multiple schedules, attending to the scraped knees and hurt feelings that blossom like wild yucca plants on the skin and in the hearts of adults and kids alike. It appears chaotic from the outside, but I promise you from the very bottom of my soul that it is tempered on the inside with love — our Greatest Commandment — for God and for one another.

Joy and anguish were central themes of those 23 years of marriage and family bonds, and they were always galvanized with *love*. It was fitting to have our first book titled *Love in the House* and, indeed, all our books following ended up with "love" it their titles. Wendy and I still feel like we're in our twenties, and I still hum along to Sammy Hagar "Why Can't This Be Love?" What happens, then, when *hate* makes an appearance on stage right of our family's loving life? You're about to find out, because facing that hate nearly ruined me, my marriage, and my family.

Love didn't seem to be enough to prepare us for October 2, 2014.

The Jeub Family in 2007, the year we appeared on television. We followed the show with a message of *Love in the House*, the title of our first book for families.

Chapter 2: Our Smear

On October 2, 2014, one of our daughters published an article on her blog that accused Wendy and me of abuse. Since we were now "TV personalities," the story spread quickly through social media and even to supermarket tabloids. "House of Horrors," one sensational-minded rag proclaimed, labeling our daughter a brave whistleblower who "escaped" from a home of hate. It appeared at first that all of our adult children — four daughters and my first-born son at the time — validated the accusation. Two at least were in full support of their sister's initial blog post and those that followed.

That first blog post was hideously false, but it changed our family forever. Our beloved daughter insisted we "pulled the curtains" every night, lined all of the children along the wall, and whipped their bottoms with belts, 50 lashings each. Our oldest daughter — the one still estranged from our family — was the first to chime in online, writing, "I'm so sorry, so, so sorry that it didn't stop." Nearly every day for the next several months, blog post after blog post continued to detail all sorts of abuses, supported by the band of siblings. The narrative was that Wendy and I fabricated an image of a perfect family in order to hide our sadistic tendencies to abuse our children.

The truth — that we do not nor ever have abused our children — eventually came out, but the initial smearing and the years that followed remains the most painful journey of our lives. The chorus of unison among the adult siblings quickly deteriorated, but it mattered little to the growing online following — the "mob" to those who understand social smearing — who refused to believe anything other than the awful, abusive "house of horrors" narrative of the Jeubs. We were, in their judgment, a secret cult of a family that manipulated little children. And how do you suppose I could have defended my family? I had daughters accusing me of something I did not do, and any attempt to defend our family name was immediately perceived as an attack on *them*, my own daughters. Why would they lie? And why would a father openly accuse them of doing so? Most people reasoned that there must be at least *some* truth to the accusations, at the very least hidden dysfunction that would cause such turmoil. Perhaps the Jeubs weren't *always* as bad as their daughters claimed, but they're definitely not the picture-perfect family they think they are. Surely, at least some shame on the Jeubs was justified.

Those who have experienced social smearing can instantly relate to how hopeless such a situation seems. The online world wants swift judgment, and only a seedy headline or two is needed to formulate a hasty condemnation. Of course, life is so much more complicated than any headline can manage to articulate. But no deeper explanation can head off the social mob that comes after you, especially when the fabrication involves whipping little children. The shock of the accusation alone will bring a prejudiced response, and how can anyone blame them? Innocent children deserve protection, so, true or not, accused abusers should be shamed.

We were posting fun photos of our big happy family one day, fighting accusations of felony-level abuse the next. Proving guilt is not required for social warriors, safely sitting behind their keyboards or furtively staring at their phones. The accusation alone does the lasting damage, and the more shocking the claim is, the more damage it will bring. It's no wonder charges are amped up to make the impossible seem possible. We don't "pull the curtains" in our home; we don't even have curtains in our front window. Fifty lashes with a belt for each of 16 children? Eight hundred of them every night? Infeasible. Impractical. Impossible. And we would allow television cameras in our home ... *to cover it up?* A moment's thought exposes the absurdity of the claims.

Absurd claims are scrutinized and questioned in a court of law, but routinely rewarded online. The damage to our family has never been reversed. The trauma extends to our friends and extended family members, to our neighbors and community, to our business and customers we associate with. It has been six years since the smear, and those who followed the story closely have come around to realize the fabrications behind the claims. But many others didn't read any further. They wrote us off as a strange, maybe even dangerous family worthy of either indifference or hatred, possibly prosecution; and that's where we stand in the eyes of many, even today.

Family life even for small families can be complicated, which makes them susceptible to a targeted pounce from inside the fort. For us, a family with 16 children, life couldn't be any *more* complicated. In many ways, Wendy and I always sought to bring clarity to the complication by writing books and blog posts and speaking to families who likewise sought order within the chaos of large-family living. Our social smear capitalized on the complication and slandered us as unstable, crazy fanatics who deserved every ounce of shame we faced online.

The purpose of this book is to deal with social smearing, ours coming from those we love. What was going on in our family in 2014 was complicated, but there were, eventually, many blessings that came from it. Understanding our family trauma will not only help you build (or rebuild) faith in our family, but I hope it will also show you that an online smear doesn't need to be the *only* narrative for anyone suffering from it.

If you are someone who already holds us in contempt, either from reading about us in the past, or maybe just from picking up this book, I want you to continue reading anyway. The "other side" was never articulated like it will be now. The socially smeared seldom have their day in court. The greater story here is in how we handled this modern phenomenon of social smearing, which is what I hope you end up learning about. We live in a world where none of us are immune, but we all have the power to overcome.

As I mentioned, it appeared our five adult children at the time were all "in" on this. That was claimed early on, but it wasn't true. My son was solicited by the others, but he bravely resisted. This was important, because much of the original accusation had him as the most abused victim; claims including beatings from his mother, who is half his size. Almost immediately he countered his sisters' story. They had hoped he would jump in with them, but he did not.

The raw immediacy of a social smear is hard to fathom. Ours was a surprise attack, shocking all of us to our cores. When attacks come from within a family, especially a loving family, your first inclination is not to counterattack publicly. Confused and dazed, you quickly reach out, groping for the meaning of it all, which is what we did. It appeared to some as hesitation or, worse, a silent admission of guilt. And when my son also hesitated, online observers accused him of being weak and revealing. But it was shock and a deep unwillingness to quarrel in front of the whole world, not guilt, that was guiding our actions. So we reached out to our accusers privately. We honestly hoped they would talk with us and abandon the nonsense of this new narrative. We were being lambasted by online strangers so much and so quickly that we were forced to turn off our social media altogether. We were much more concerned for the health of our family than we were about our online reputation, and we assumed that our daughters were, too.

They weren't.

The awkward predicament of social smearing from those we love is that your silence — even when chosen to minimize the potential damage arguing could do to everyone in your family, including those members who are doing the accusing — is perceived by the online world as guilt. What, people asked, did we have to say to the accusations? Were they true or not? Why not just try to clear the air? *Do you or do you not beat your children?* The online mob sees these questions as reasonable. While your head is still spinning like a runaway Tilt-A-Whirl, the megaphone of online media is demanding that you explain yourself.

We did finally give such a defense a feeble shot. But it did little to convince the online mob of our innocence. I used to run a podcast for academic speakers and debaters, part of my family's business of publishing debate materials for junior high and high school competitors. The podcast was a small niche, approximately 100 listeners a day. I had been publicly accused of a crime, so I reasoned that my small audience, at least, needed to hear an answer from me. So I asked four of my older children — all competitors in the speech and debate events that my podcast catered to — into my office with microphones. I left the room, and they responded, using their own words, to the online smearing from their older siblings. Hearing it later, I thought their reasoning to be clear, collected and thorough; and I had hoped it would put the matter to rest.

I would soon learn that heartfelt explanation is not on the radar of social shamers, nor is the truth. More than 4,000 listeners tuned into our podcast the only day it was up. And they all heard our eldest son explain his side of the abuse allegations, countering the details and specifics of his sisters' claims. This helped reduce the magnitude of the claim: We were no longer a family of nightly beatings, but a family that had an embarrassing evening years before. Allow me to reveal our embarrassment: The event that our son explained was from four years prior, on an evening when I was away and Wendy was frustrated over my son's repeated refusal to help with the dishes. In perhaps her most untempered action ever toward her children — in this case, a husky teenage son taller and much bigger than she — Wendy heaved a tray of silverware in his general direction. The blog made it sound as if she came after him with hunting knives. Honestly, my children laughed when sharing the story, also recalling how Wendy apologized for her lack of civility. Was it uncivil? Of course. Was it abusive? Not even close.

Even that story, though, was reason enough for the full-throated judgment of the online world. In their minds we still deserved the condemnation and the shame. We took the podcast down, but someone from the online mob republished it on YouTube, and the harassment continued.

There is no hiding from the online world when it decides to sink its teeth into you.

This is a sad reality of the social smearer, one that I hope you take careful note of. You may be a reasonable person who wishes to resolve conflict and realize the truth in complicated situations, but the online mob does not. I have seen others jump onto the internet and lash back at their accusers. I've seldom seen good outcomes, especially when they lash out at relatives or close friends who are smearing them. The result is sometimes a hornets' nest of outraged haters, and the only ones who have the stomach to keep in the fight are those haters. Reasonable people leave, exhausted and abused.

Social smearing is a rapidly growing reality today, but it was relatively unknown in 2014. Still, the night following our daughter's initial post, we were visited by friends who had already experienced social smearing in their own way. A year prior, they had lost one of their daughters when she took shelter under a bridge during a flash flood. Recent fires made such flooding even more dangerous than usual, and their daughter became a tragic victim. Yet even they faced online shaming. Rather than expressing sympathy for the mourning parents, online opinionators confronted them with questions about their parental judgment in allowing their teenager to go for a walk in the afternoon. "What kind of idiots" (the actual words of one keyboard warrior) would tell their daughter to take shelter? Such cruelty. Our friends came to comfort us, knowing full well what we were experiencing. They even said they suspected our pain was greater than theirs since the attacks were not coming from strangers, but from our own children.

Comfort also came when some of our friends took it upon themselves to stand up for us. One was like a daughter to us, who grew up as a close neighbor and friend to our family. Online, she sharply criticized my daughters for their fabrications. If anyone knew of abuse, she would be the one, she said. But the online mob cared little for her arguments. She eventually shut it off. Our family counselor, too, came to our defense online, especially after my daughters claimed she knew of past abuse. This was untrue, and she made it clear that such defamation was wrong and illegal.

The online mob ridiculed her for surrendering doctor-patient privilege (which she did not). But she, too, eventually shut it off. Countless others who had connections with our daughters attempted to reach out to them online, but they had the mob to back them up as they continued to insist our home was a home of abuse. Sometimes our defenders ended up in my daughter's next blog post, as she shamed them, often by name, for "enabling" the imagined abuse. In the end, at least in the short term, each of our stalwart character witnesses was forced off the online discussion.

Most brokenhearted were the rest of my children. They were straw-manned as "brainwashed" by their mastermind parents, weak victims who needed to break free from us like their brave sisters had. My second-born son, just a year younger than my first and nearly an adult, was most devastated. He had a strong story of overcoming severe dyslexia and going on to winning national speech tournaments. He's quite a success story, but his sisters hijacked his story to accuse us of "educational abuse," making his dyslexia somehow our failure as parents. He hated the misrepresentation and attempted to enter the online frenzy to set things straight. He was teased by his sisters, especially when he would misspell words, and the online community claimed such misspellings as evidence of our "educational abuse," not his dyslexia. My son, too, withdrew.

I tried to read the posts as they came out. I felt like I needed to, no matter how emotionally exhausting they became. Every time my daughter referenced me as an abuser, which every post did, it was like a dagger to my heart. I kept hoping for her to explain a deeper pain or a reason for her lashing out, perhaps a glimmer of hope for a relationship that could be mended. This eventually came from her sisters, but it never came from her. Our relationship used to be so, so strong, and I couldn't imagine why she was advocating such a vile narrative of her childhood. I would lay in bed, desperately fighting off deep depression, remembering how we used to travel the country together, enter speech and debate tournaments, share old vinyl records from my youth, and work on developing her writing career and education through her blog. There were so many grand memories, but they were all being wiped away and replaced with a false memory of abuse, neglect and trauma. Overnight, our beautiful life together became an online mockery. We were publicly beaten in the streets of online media.

I also withdrew. I had to.

Today I find it very difficult to justify any social smearing, even smearing that ends up being true. Social smearing is meant to defame, not solve a crime. There is something cruelly unjust about an accusation made public, as opposed to subpoenaed by a state magistrate. Real abusers should be tested in court, not the corridors of online sensationalism. There, they have their day of defense and, if found guilty, are brought to justice. But those of us who are innocent rarely get our day in court. And the defamation we face continues to do its damage as the years unwind. Our accusers know that.

Social smearers live in a surreal online world, while the rest of us reside in reality. So, living in the real world, Wendy and I fully expected our world's magistrate — who is, in the case of familial abuse, a Child Protection Services social worker — to show up at our door to investigate. Our daughters posted online about how they had called upon such a CPS officer "several times." We got a lawyer and taped his card to our calendar, and we had his number speed dialed into our phones. Grimly, we braced ourselves for the worst possible interrogation, but I recall secretly hoping to end up in court. At least there my daughters could testify; the rest of my children could, too, along with friends and family. My name would finally be cleared and my family would have the chance to rebuild.

But CPS never knocked. I doubt they were ever called, not by my daughters or the mob that followed them. I now see this as a common practice for those who seek defamation rather than justice: Posting online without following with an investigation does much more harm to the victims than seeking a just trial. In other words, the online world does much greater damage than the legal world, and smearers know it. My daughters knew their siblings were not in danger, so calling the authorities would only bring scrutiny to their claims of such. We faced the audience of online hate rather than the magistrate of the state. I suppose that if we were guilty of abuse we'd prefer to avoid the latter. But we were innocent, so I claim the former as worse.

What would you do in my situation? I wanted so badly for this to end, but every attempt to bring reconciliation or even just an old-fashioned truce was used against me. Would you have reached out? Of course you would have, just as I did. My daughters blocked my phone number, social media messages and emails. Would you have then posted on their social media profiles? I did, but it only served as "evidence" of my so-called control issues. Every attempt to connect was seen as weakness and/or manipulation, and often my sincere words ended up as damning quotes for future blog posts.

Later in the month we celebrated the birthday of our twins. They were young, kept from the drama of the online smear, and we were hoping their older siblings would drop their online guard. I reached out in a private message, sent from an alias email account so that I knew they would receive it. It read:

> Hi girls. I wanted to extend an invitation to attend our traditional powwow with the twins tonight. We're having sherbet floats at 7pm, and you are welcome to join us.
>
> Know that the twins know nothing cf your articles or of the emotional trouble any of us are experiencing. We unanimously agreed that you will be welcome for our little private party. We hope you can make it tonight. The twins will most assuredly welcome you.
>
> Same rules apply as already mentioned: no pulling kids aside for any private conversations. It would be nice to keep social media out of this, too. This is merely to honor the twins and our love for them. We hope to see you tonight.
>
> We love you,
>
> Dad

I was careful about this, even sharing the email with one of our lawyers. Please understand: We were fearful of social services paying us a visit, of them taking our children away during an investigation. Our adult children were already doing all they could to impugn us of vile crimes. We wanted reconciliation so badly, wanted to try to understand their rage and hatred, and if a simple birthday party would help move everyone closer to that, we were all for it.

One of the girls responded with a terse and cold, "Not interested."

October 24, the day following our party, the next blog post dropped. It was titled, "I'm Sorry You Lost Your Kids." In it, my daughter took the role of the "better parent" and started to claim that we were keeping her siblings from her and that we were lying to them about her:

> These days, I drive past my parents' house and there's a dull ache in me. Those kids were mine. I raised them, and I can't see them. Sure, I could drop in uninvited, but it would do no good. My little brothers and sisters have been trained to distrust and hate me, just as I was taught to hate my older sisters.
>
> It's like I've lost custody of my kids, except I was the better parent, and the court never asked about my rights. Also the parents who got to keep my kids are abusive, and they tell lies about me.

She wasn't driving by. None of them were. They were invited, they were welcome, and they weren't being lied about. The twins were too young to know, and we kept hoping this would all blow over before they ever needed to. We never guessed this would last for years to come.

In the weeks and months and years that followed, Wendy and I largely turned off the rest of the world. She deleted her Facebook app from her phone and refused any attempt from strangers to contact her. For a while I stepped in and filtered her email, deleting the mean ones and showing her the supportive ones. I consider myself stronger in filtering through the trolls, but even I was growing more and more depressed. Even though my business required a strong social media presence, I ended up ignoring it more and more, and then, finally, turning it off altogether. I let all the hate pile up online while I turned my heart toward what was left of my big, beautiful family.

My instincts still told me to defend my family, but experience had taught me it was foolish to do it online. I was ready to give up all of my online presence to save my family from the ongoing trauma of this social smear. I turned inward, seeking counsel from professionals, friends and family, and began to painstakingly decipher a path forward that eventually would make us stronger than ever. It was a long and torturous journey, and we are still walking it in many ways. But the walk has brought about blessings that we would not have realized without the pain. Let me tell you about my family's first tentative steps toward healing in the next chapter.

It is easy to become defensive when lies are being spread about you, but we've learning to "lean in" on the fabrications and discover the hidden truths in them.

This picture was taken on one of our quests in Melbourne, Australia.

Chapter 3: Lean In

I've thought many times recently about my own adolescent hatred toward my father. "I hate you, Dad!" was my none-too-subtle truth, shouted to his face in my time of immaturity. I knew he loved me, but I routinely returned his love with hatred. I walled him off, pushing him from my life. I rejected any attempt he made to connect or reconnect. Today teens flip on their cell phone and text their friends. In the 1980s we ran to the second telephone in the house. At risk of being heard through the walls or my dad picking up the main line, I would call my friend across my little town and complain of the injustices I suffered in my home. He'd do the same, and our social network of two would have it out.

The phone on the wall. This simple networking limitation calmed countless family turmoils, no doubt. To my dad's credit, he and I would often follow up with a less tense conversation, as I hope happens in most families. Fights flare up and are then doused between siblings and spouses in just the same way. I can't say that the phone line to my friend helped any, other than perhaps allowing both of us the time to process the fights we were having with our parents. My dad didn't forbid me to call my friend. In retrospect, I realize that he let the "I hate you" moment hang in the air, allowed me the time to vent in the other room, and he probably spent time venting himself. We were free to let time and further conversation heal our wounds.

Today the phone no longer sits locked to a wall. It lives, everpresent, in our pocket. Not one line to one friend, but the internet to the world. We have social media, blogs and even the mainstream media hungry for a juicy story to share with *everyone*. How could my dad and I ever have come back to a wholesome conversation if my social network extended beyond the phone on my wall, to a world of haters who would have banded with me to support and solidify my hatred toward my dad at that moment?

Social smearing is a Pandora's box of our modern times. I'll bet you could share some stories, couldn't you? Bitter spouses now use social smearing as their weapon of choice before divorcing. A surefire way to stay separated from a sibling is to post defaming truths online. Schools typically have shared Facebook groups that are supposed to be a community of parents, but they're often hijacked by those who use it to criticize every move made by the school board or any teacher or administrator. Coworkers, neighbors, churches — a smartphone and social media can ruin a reputation, a relationship or a livelihood in one viral post. Your story may have unique aspects to it, but social smearing is a most common dilemma of the modern world.

Escape is a natural reaction to a social smear. "Get me outta here!" follows a swarm of haters coming at you to shame you. We did this in the first six months of our day-by-day smearing. We traveled to Oklahoma, Minnesota and even Australia. But these trips weren't merely about hiding from our problems. All three helped solve familial issues that we were having extreme trouble sorting out. Sorting out truth from fiction. And learning how to "lean in" to the hate. Turns out the mountain-like problems that seemed impossible to move did have embedded answers that helped us plot a plan of eventual escape.

Before our social smear went viral, Wendy and I had scheduled speaking engagements at four conferences in America and one in Canada. All five terminated in uncomfortable conversations with the hosts asking to drop us from their program. We were so emotionally exhausted, we meekly accepted being let go from their schedules.

But we still traveled. First, off to Oklahoma we went. I had a deal with another publisher that was interested in acquiring my smaller publishing company at the time. I had already planned a trip to visit them and take care of business. Wendy was home with the kids, afraid that any day a social worker or police officer would visit. As I already explained, that day never came, but my beloved wife's fear of facing it without me brought tremendous anxiety. So we loaded the kids in the van and took off to Oklahoma together.

This telling centers on the social smearing of my family, of course, but something should be noted about friendships. My family was walking through a devastating trauma of horrendous magnitude, and I do not believe many other families could have withstood it. I'm not saying we're special in some mystically supersonic way, but we do have an unusually enormous number of friends and caring families who surround us. This short sojourn was a business trip, but it afforded us time to visit friends whose children grew up with mine, a family that had just recently moved to Oklahoma. I cannot tell you how therapeutic it is to stay up late with dear friends and talk through the pains of family drama.

That's not to say all of our friends knew what to say. We had close friends who attempted to sympathize, but didn't have it within their social abilities to help. I remember one friend asking what I did wrong to get my daughters to slander us so much. "You must have done something!" he insisted. Another kept reminding me that I had "plenty of other blessings" around the house, meaning my other children. This comment was intended to comfort me, but it tore at my bleeding heart. A third insisted that I should just call up my daughters and express my love for them, then everything would be okay. As if I hadn't already tried.

My business partner had to eventually pull out of the publishing acquisition, but that decision didn't reflect his genuine understanding of what my family and I were going through. He related, having a daughter who likewise had done some social smearing of her own. She and her stepmom — my friend's wife — do not get along. And the daughter doesn't keep her opinion to herself, to say the least. She would gossip about her stepmom, ridicule her in front of other relatives, and attempt to shame her through their social media channels. It was hardly to the magnitude of my social smearing, but my friend was still able to sincerely empathize with my trials. I very much appreciated his friendship.

Parents who have lost their children to death will often tell of the need to leave the premises, sometimes selling their home and moving out of town. I get it. Everything around the house reminded us of our older children. It wasn't just the house; it was our small town, too. Wendy and I even felt embarrassed to make simple errands, fearing someone would see us, knowing that we were accused abusers. Our white van proudly displayed 18 stick figure silhouettes, and we now wanted to scrape them from our window. Going to the grocery store took emotional focus, so you can see why taking off to Oklahoma was a nice escape.

The trip helped, but it didn't solve everything. My daughters continued to rage against Wendy and me, also turning on their siblings and extended relatives. Those siblings and relatives would try to reach out to them, but they would return their love with biting hatred, sometimes making them the subjects of their blogging fabrications. They had blocked my emails and phone calls, so I was tempted to engage them online. I didn't. I had learned that I couldn't. And slowly our network of friends and family began abandoning them. (My daughters replaced them with people who knew little of our family or had never met us personally.) We don't know for sure, but I suspect most people — even some of our friends — initially believed the accusation of abuse, but eventually subsided when there was no other testimony other than that of this small band of sisters. A whistleblower typically empowers others to come forward, but no one did. You'd think that a "mastermind abuser" like me would have a history of abuse witnessed by relatives, friends and neighbors throughout the years. Yet no one — not one person — validated any of my daughters' claims.

If you think this made me feel any better, think again. I was suffering such severe depression by this point that I was physically immobile at times.

I'd never felt this down-and-out before, my knees aching when I managed to get out of bed in the morning, hesitating to carry out the simplest of tasks. Wendy pulled most of the weight around the home, and our children pitched in, seeming to be much more resilient than me. They seemed to somehow be acclimated to resisting the online smear. I would peek and read the latest post or jump on Facebook hoping to see a friendly comment, only to be utterly let down and depressed. It was an ugly cycle that I found very difficult to break.

Our second trip was at the end of November. The prospect of a CPS visit was becoming more and more distant, but the house still haunted us. So we loaded up the 15-passenger van again and took off to Minnesota for Thanksgiving. My parents own a home that they built over a decade before, largely with my family in mind. The upstairs was where they lived, but the basement — fully furnished with bathroom, two bedrooms and a living room — was perfect for our large family to sprawl out. Cousins would join my children downstairs, while my sisters and Wendy's, too, would visit upstairs. It made for a wonderful vacation.

Extended relatives handled our situation differently. I got tremendous support from my oldest sister, a school counselor with a masters in psychology. The parent of one child, she had always found my family rather fascinating, and she loved to psychoanalyze our family drama, spending hours talking through the dynamics of our large family. My youngest sister at first seemed to sympathize with my daughters, but she eventually dropped her support. I most feared I was going to lose my third sister over all of this. She was the same sister who introduced me to Wendy, but we had had a shaky relationship ever since my marriage. She and I seldom agreed on anything, and I knew her to be quick to judge any situation that I was in. I assumed she would not be supportive of me, perhaps even encouraging the online attacks against my family.

I slowly learned from her to not make assumptions on who knows what, how much they may judge my situation, or that they wouldn't be able to identify with my pain. This is an important perspective to have when facing hate. You don't know what you don't know — or, rather, what other people know or don't know — and you need to develop an attitude of "ignorance" as you face new and old acquaintances in day-to-day life. I wish I would have figured this out sooner in processing my social smear. It has robbed me of much joy as I assumed others' judgment of me and my situation. The fact was, I didn't know. Sometimes I would be surprised at how understanding, sympathetic and caring other people were to my unique situation.

Such was the case with my sister, who, I learned, had experienced a social smear of her own. Years earlier, she had divorced and remarried a man with grown children. One of his adult children smeared my sister to the rest of her family, making her out to be the "wicked stepmother" of their blended family. This was an unfair humiliation of my sister, but one that gave her a fair amount of empathy toward my situation. I had anticipated her blaming my large family, my Christian faith, or even my wife for my daughters' rebellion. She didn't, staunchly expressing her understanding and support. She reminded me that she had grown up with me and knew I was not the abuser my daughters claimed me to be. She was a strong encouragement to me in the first months following our smear.

Do you see a thread woven through my trips? It was becoming clear that many of our friends and family identified with the trial we were going through, much more than I would have guessed. Those of us who face online ridicule and shaming seem to believe we are alone in our problems. We aren't as alone as we think. Even back then there were others already dealing with online smearing.

We usually visit just family in our trips to Minnesota, but this time an old friend made a concerted effort to connect with me during our stay, bringing her children and husband on a two-hour drive to eat leftover turkey with us on the Saturday of Thanksgiving weekend. Normally, reconnecting with such an old friend would have been joyous, but my worry over whether she knew that I was accused of abuse haunted me. She was, after all, a social worker and former Child Protective Services agent, and though we had been friends since high school, I was afraid our friendship would be compromised if she knew. I must admit that I stewed over this dilemma long enough to let paranoia set in.

It turned out that she knew everything, and had been reading the online accusations. After dinner I asked her straight up, "Do you know what I'm going through right now?" "Of course," she said. It was all over social media. In fact, she had been approached by friends not as close to me as she was, inquiring about it all. This is what caused her to contact me and want to get together with my family during our visit to Minnesota. Perhaps it was her own little private investigation, but it turned out to be a tremendous encouragement. As a former CPS agent she had dealt with the worst of the worst of families, severe abuse victims of unimaginable proportions. "Chris, you and Wendy are not abusers," she affirmed, "and any CPS worker with half a brain would see right through this."

It also became clear that my friend was quite familiar with stories like mine. As social media become more and more of a central force in family dynamics, stories like mine — and my Oklahoma friends', my business partner's and my sister's — were no longer as uncommon as I had thought. "Adult children grow up and lash out at their parents, always have. Today they use social media to do their damage," my friend told me. "Most real abuse victims are embarrassed by the abuse, or they are at least smart enough to know that going public on social media will do nothing to help their situation." Good point, I thought. She then closed the case: "You and Wendy are obviously not abusers, Chris. Sitting here in your parents' home, my kids playing with your kids, and seeing the love abound in you and your family is something the families I see can only dream of. We social workers are much too busy helping genuinely abusive families."

What an affirming visit this was. Connecting with my sisters and my old friend went a long way toward soothing my aching soul, pummeled as it was from the social smearing that I was experiencing. And I fervently hope it encourages you to also connect with your loved ones whenever you find yourself being raked over online coals. Don't assume *everyone* is against you, because chances are that they are, actually, *for you*. Perhaps, like me, you will find some of the most empathetic people to be those you mistakenly judged to be your adversaries. It is very sweet to find close friends and family on your side.

I was accused of felony-level abuse, which was untrue. Stunned and shocked, I was not flatly denying it at the time, but I do so today with confident affirmation. What about social smearing that *is* true, though? What about claims that aren't felony-level? What if, let's say, my daughters had chosen to blog about how I have lost my temper at times, raised my voice at the dinner table, or some other irritating-yet-legal behavior? In fact, my daughters did start blogging about such things as spankings, as well as vague accusations of "spiritual" and "emotional" abuse. Their online narrative moved away from allegations of illegal beatings to the more mundane private family interactions and altercations that are routine and obviously *legal,* yet still embarrassing when bantered about in public.

In the social media world, such smears are much more common. Not many of us are accused of patently illegal behavior, but you may have been smeared for past moral failures. Someone somewhere witnessed you acting out, getting drunk, being ornery, untempered, angry, whatever. All of us fail morally in some capacity, and if those around us who were offended or hurt from the situation chose ill will as their response, they can do great damage to you by going on an online rampage. I sometimes think my daughters would have done greater damage to me and my reputation if they blogged about how much of a jerk I can be sometimes. Because the truth is, I *can* be a jerk! I wouldn't have been able to defend myself.

Shame on those who turn to online smearing to dig into others' weaknesses and shortcomings! Even true whistleblowers suffering from illegal abuse or corruption should studiously avoid the online arena when airing their cases, but at least one can understand why they might be tempted to take that route. There is *no* excuse for disgruntled people digging into others for all-too-human failures. This is a common tide now that is swelling to tsunami proportions, and for the sake of our civilization we need to reverse it. I'll get into how to do this later in the book, but I want to tell you how my story surfaced a solution for those of us accused of secret sins:

Lean in.

Granted, it is unfair that you are being smeared online for your past behavior, but still lean in and receive the "shaming" as diplomatically as you can. This takes delicate maneuvering if you're being attacked by a loved one, but it's the best way to address any embarrassing-but-true smear. This is different than slander, which are falsities and fabrications being told about you with the purpose to do harm. I'm talking here of gossip, still used to do you harm, but stemming from truths about you. I encourage you to lean in on the truth of the matter by accepting the critique and humbly seeking the truth in it as you learn from it. Your adversary is publicly exposing a weakness in you, and that's painfully wrong. But when you lean in, rejecting the method of smearing while owning up to what you did, you end up overcoming the intent of the hatred. Such a maneuver will at the very least make you a better person. At most, it will also win back the heart of your accuser.

This has been a significant discussion in my family, and our visit to Minnesota unearthed a lot of reflection on how we were raised, how we previously raised our older children, and how we were currently raising the brood still in our home. Both Wendy and I were children of the 1970s and '80s, and the dispensement of parental discipline was handled much differently in our homes than it generally is now. As adults, my dad and I have had deep discussions of his harsher use of corporal punishment, and it helped mold my milder use of the same. And I must say here that through the course of my 30 years of parenting, I have changed my methods of child rearing and have become what I believe to be a stable, even-keeled dad who disciplines with a "rod of correction" that doesn't always include physical spankings.

Early in my parenting venture I was a student of Dr. James Dobson's *Dare to Discipline,* as well as other authors who articulated how to lovingly and properly exercise corporal punishment. As time went on, I've come to believe (and Wendy agrees) that the key principle in all psychological use of negative reinforcement is *practice.* Whenever a child "acts up," Wendy and I began striving to, first, keep our tempers, and then craft a "practice session" designed to teach proper behavior through repetition. Most traditional forms of corrective discipline — yelling, time-outs, spankings, taking away toys, and even shaming — do little to actually teach *new* behavior. They must be combined — or even replaced at times — with this idea of "practice."

It was a liberating revelation for Wendy and me early in our family life together. Like many parents, especially parents of multiple children, we were overwhelmed with the nearly constant need to discipline our kids. "Practicing" proper behavior was a saving grace for our family — right about the time we were contemplating serious birth control to stop the madness! — that encouraged us to continue having more children. The idea of spending the rest of our lives running after a gaggle of little hellions to give them a good lickin' for each of their bad actions would have driven me to a vasectomy long ago. Instead of a large happy family, we would have had a small, miserable one!

I don't bring this up to preach to you about how to discipline your children, nor to give some political statement on corporal punishment. My point is simply that families need to *talk* about these things, not to tear each other down but to build each other up. I don't talk with my dad about his harsher mid-'80s disciplinary techniques to shame him for not parenting like a dad might four decades later. If I went online and shamed my dad for that which he did 40 years ago — things that were widely considered to be perfectly appropriate, mind you — the shame should be on me. (Even to talk about him in this book, I asked his permission.) I prefer an atmosphere of love and acceptance, which allows us to grow from our past experiences, becoming better people and parents. We all need to be allowed the grace to *lean in* on those places where we are weak, learn from them, and become better for it.

Why, then, would my daughter fabricate a narrative that wasn't hers? At the time this didn't make any sense to me. Why would any of my children, raised in a functional, loving home by parents who worked hard at breaking dysfunctional chains, invent stories of abuse merely to smear their parents?

The answer was revealed in our third trip.

There is a profound connection between my daughter who started the online smear and her sister who moved to Australia three years prior. She met a young Muslim man from Syria and had gone on to marry him. Included in the online smear was the notion that we "kicked her out" and ostracized her from the family for their Muslim faith, but none of it was remotely true. She was being solicited by her sisters to join in on the online social smear, but, like her brother, she refused. So the apparent bond of five siblings at the beginning of our drama was actually just three. And even that trio's pact, thankfully, eventually began to wither.

Nearly two months into our social smear that continued online, we felt the overwhelming conviction to connect with our Aussie-residing daughter. She had gone through a time of angry rebellion against us — particularly against her mother — that left her reeling in her early adulthood. She, like her sisters, wandered restlessly, looking for purpose elsewhere, even to another faith and another country on the other side of the planet. She, too, shared a story of abuse as a child, but she didn't post it online as a social smear. Instead, she shared it with her sisters with the assumption that they would keep it private among themselves. So in a way, her sisters were publicly retelling the stories that she told in private, and this left her feeling betrayed and embarrassed.

Remember, Wendy and I have 16 children. We've parented them differently through the years, and we confess (as virtually all parents of multiple children confess), that we were the hardest on the oldest. Early in our parenting we treated spanking like a science, studying the technique and applying it judiciously. We never spanked in anger, using it as simple correction for misbehavior. Our daughter was most certainly what Dr. Dobson would have called a "strong-willed child" (of which he so eloquently wrote in his bestseller *The Strong-Willed Child*). As such, I regret to say now, she faced more spankings than she truly deserved.

Lining her and her siblings up along the wall and whipping with belts was never true, but emotionally, in her inner child's mind's eye, it was her recollection of her past. She would argue with her younger siblings, saying things like, "Oh, you have no idea how good you have it now …," followed with sometimes humorously exaggerated tales of the "horrors" she suffered. The conversation ended up being portrayed in a much worse light online later, becoming a core part of the social smearing that we've suffered.

By the end of our earlier weekend in Minnesota, we had connected over Skype with our daughter and her husband in Australia. Though we hadn't yet met him in person, he had already shown a tremendous amount of support for Wendy and me in our situation. But this issue — the idea that we might have "abused" her when she was little — seemed to be a focal point for the larger story. Coupled with the fact that this daughter was extremely close to her older sister who seemed to be clinging to the online narrative of our felony-level abuse, there was something relationally significant that needed to be explored.

I had to lean in on the truth of that accusation, humbly accept the part for which I could accept blame without surrendering to the shame of exaggeration. So while still in Minnesota we secured two plane tickets to Australia and we scheduled a spring break in Melbourne. My parents were huge helps, financing one of the plane tickets and traveling to Colorado to babysit the children. Our trip correlated with our daughter's golden birthday — 29 years old on March 29th — making this a coincidental blessing in our healing process.

Of our 16 children, she was our strongest-willed. I suppose conflicts between parents and strong-willed children is reason for many estrangements, but for us the pain transformed into a beautiful reconciliation that empowered all of us. In visiting our daughter and son-in-law — staying in their small apartment together for two weeks — many rich conversations explored deep meanings in our adult relationship. Tensions existed in the past, but hatred was not among them, and judgment is stomped out with love anytime its ugliness appears.

We very much enjoyed this time in Australia, the four of us eating, sightseeing and sharing together, without any children to tow around for a change! Blogging about our trip, I focused on my 25-year relationship with our strong-willed daughter, especially how we previously had tried to change her strong will through discipline. I explained one story where she insisted on walking 10 miles to daycare as a five-year-old, one of those "strong-willed moments" that we both recall today with laughter. I ended the post with this:

> I guess you can say I'm ashamed of the fact that I made her strong will a shameful thing. If I could rewind time, I would have reacted differently. I would have made a picnic out of her insistence that she could walk 10 miles to daycare. I would have tried to walk to daycare with her, then allowed her to give up when her little legs got the best of her. Who knows, maybe she would have surprised the family after all and made it all the way. I think, at 29 years old, she still believes she could have made it. Still so stubborn!
>
> Today, her insistence on love has been a true blessing for our family. She won't submit to family turmoil others may try to push on her. She is relentless about love, never betraying a confidence, and stubborn about it. I've learned long ago not to try to manipulate her or get her to do something she doesn't want to do.
>
> In retrospect, her strong will was a gift I should have cultivated more than resisted.

Let me talk directly to those of you who are facing social smearing from family members — or any kind of hateful attack from a loved one — take time to pause and consider what you can learn from the attack. Lean in. Chances are good that there is something you can learn, and if you embrace it, you will become a better person because of it. I believe Wendy and I are much, much better parents today than we were in the 1990s when we were just starting out. And I am incredibly grateful that our daughter, now so far away in Australia, gave us the patience we needed to accept her grievances and allow us to grow.

Three trips brought me these gifts: Empathy from my business partner and sister, justification from my psychologist sister and old friend, humility from my parents and understanding from my adult daughter. All of these connections helped me escape from the emotional trap of my social smear by diving deeper into a human level apart from the court of public opinion and that of the mob. And that act of diving deeper raised me up to a higher realization of my life and the love of those around me. My online experience was truly one of walking through the valley of the shadow of death, and I suppose the rest of the watching world thought I was shamed and humiliated and destitute. I wasn't. In a way, I was being "born again" to a more pure spiritual understanding of the realities of my life and the relationships I hold dear.

But don't let me overstate. Though these trips were wonderfully liberating to me emotionally, I still was a virtual prisoner to my social smear. Online I was a vicious abuser of little children, as my three daughters locked arms and unified their testimony against me. Though I never had my day in court, I sat confined in my cell of condemnation, and it appeared that I was in this prison for life. I needed to plot my escape, but wasn't certain how. You will see in the coming chapters that my escape came from the most unusual places.

Those of us who face online ridicule and shaming seem to believe we are alone in our problems. We aren't as alone as we think.

Photo taken at Thanksgiving dinner in Minnesota, weeks following our smear.

Chapter 4: Rush

You need to watch *The Shawshank Redemption* more than once to fully grasp its conclusion. The movie follows banker Andy Dufresne, sentenced to two consecutive life terms for the murder of his adulterous wife and her lover, of which Andy is innocent. Throughout this poignant tale, you wonder if he will ever be freed, you question whether he will convince the warden to request a retrial and you balk at the immense injustice of being forced to live out two decades of his life in a maximum security prison. Andy's mountain is truly impossible to move. At the moment of utter desperation, when you think Andy is at his end and won't be able to claw his way through this unfair tribulation, you discover that he can indeed conquer the impossible. For twenty years Andy had not depressingly succumbed to life's circumstances, as it appeared. He had been planning his escape.

Without commenting on the ethics and morality of plotting a prison break or the events that led to receiving his unjust sentence, I want to proclaim that at least Andy Dufresne *got* a trial. The socially smeared don't get such privilege. But like all the prisoners in Shawshank, we are ripped of so much that we sink deep into our miserable circumstances. The obvious for me was losing my oldest children, three of whom still held fast to the online narrative that I was an abuser who deserved a lifetime of humiliating shame. Though untrue, the public accusation alone nearly ruined me. Social smearing cripples people emotionally, financially and (of course) socially.

Going through the shock of a social smearing is overwhelming, truly a mountain impossible to budge.

Emotionally, I was a wreck. I had never been prone to depression before, but I sure was now, at times unwilling to even drag myself out of bed to do the most basic tasks. As a father and business owner, I still had much to do. But my legs were tired and my mind numb, especially at the darkest moments of my family's struggles. I had to give myself pep talks to get out of bed, follow-up pep talks to take on the day's duties, and I even recall counting the minutes till bedtime, sleep being my only true escape from my sorrow. I never understood depression before this dark time, judging it to be a sign of weakness or simply a negative attitude. It's not! And it eventually led me to seek professional help.

Financially, I nearly went bankrupt. I'm a solopreneur, meaning I run a business of which I'm the sole employee, but I depend on several others to make the whole thing work. My writers and private contractors sensed my melancholy. My business — providing source material and curriculum to academic speakers and debaters participating in various high school leagues — was a small market but had provided an income for my family for the previous dozen years. After my social smear began, revenue dropped, and Wendy and I had to provide for the family through refinancing our home and slowly sinking into debt to pay the bills.

Socially, I found myself very alone, and though most people eventually realized my innocence, no one enjoyed being close. I was a depressing presence to be around, always thinking of my daughters, their latest public jab against me and my family, not at all the "Jeub"-ulent life of the party I used to be. I wasn't invited to graduations that spring when usually my refrigerator had dozens taped to its door. Two former students of mine married the following summer, and I couldn't help but think that I should have gotten invitations. A distant cousin, whom I had developed a budding relationship with two years prior to my social smear, ended up falling off into silence. The business would have been sold that year, but it involved a three-year contract to carry its success past the acquisition. I was such a wreck that I suspect they saw its inevitable failure, so they abandoned the purchase.

The previous chapter shares a few breaks in the clouds, but those of us who suffer a significant social smear experience unfathomable losses. I believe personal ruin must be at least part of the intent of the social smearer. They either deliberately or passionately imagine your emotional depletion, financial poverty and social humiliation. Indeed, my situation appeared hopeless, an impossible mountain to move, and I could see no way out. Like Andy Dufresne, I was locked up for life, and I was doomed to fill my term for the rest of my days.

I missed my daughters, especially the one who spearheaded the blogging aspect of the smear. She was my blossoming writer, the one I helped set up her own blogging platform, the one whose skills paralleled mine in her young adult life. She was always cheerful and interested in her family, particularly her father; my one child who would explore my old vinyl records and even shared a liking for my favorite bands. Our spiritual discussions were often deep waters, and she sometimes challenged my understanding of faith in growth-minded ways. I had done what I could through my social media channels to promote her writing, even when it was edgy and might evoke pushback from my customers. Her blogging eventually turned on me, but I still would not want to dim the light she was to the world as she launched into adulthood.

This had always been the focus of my business, the one that provided an income for my growing family for years. Monument Publishing was the curriculum-selling business that published source material for speakers and debaters (and it still runs today), but the ministry — Training Minds Ministry — had been depleted to near ruin. The ministry was based on 1 Peter 1:13, which simply says, "Train the mind for action." *Action* was what I taught as the ultimate goal for anyone mastering the art of speech and debate. I wanted to see what God would do with the incredible talent that speech and debate activities produced. My disappointment was so immense that I doubted the fundamental roots of my ministry.

Today my daughter still blogs about my alleged abuse of her and her siblings. I have spent countless futile hours trying to understand her sharp turn to become the cruelest adversary of all that she used to proclaim as love and truth. Of my three daughters who still — after Australia — created the strong online bond of an untrue narrative, this one was the most vocal, the author of the blog posts and the aggressive campaigning that followed. To this day, six years later, she still holds to the initial social smearing narrative that I abuse my children. None of her family validates this.

I did have one opportunity to indirectly peer into her mind when I ran into a counterpart of hers at a debate tournament. Recall that my home business caters largely to homeschool debaters, and an alumnus of my Training Minds camps was a vocal advocate for my daughter's social smear. In the judges' lounge at a national tournament in South Carolina — a large room full of tables and chairs set up for alumni, coaches and community judges to fill out their ballots — my daughter's comrade and I coincidentally sat back to back at two separate tables. I tried to avoid her, consumed in a conversation with an extremely annoying dad of 10 children who *would not* shut up about his *perfect* kids!

Okay. I don't mean that. I truly don't. I harbor no disrespect for this dad who had ivy league adult children and was enjoying his first grandchildren. (His smile was ear to ear when he talked of his grandkids.) But my heart at the time was bleeding on the floor. I'm not sure he knew of my situation, but I don't know if he could have empathized with me even if he had. How could he? Ordinarily I would have welcomed the pleasant exchange of family updates, but my adult children weren't calling home with news of college degrees or the blessing of grandchildren — they were shaming me online and accusing me of evils I had nothing to do with. While he gushed about his joyous life, my stomach ached over my failing effort to pull my family back together.

I excused myself as cordially as I could, stood, and pushed in my chair. I turned around to leave, but my eyes met those of my daughter's online advocate, my former debate student. My body tensed. "Hi," was all I could say, "how are you?"

Please understand that at the time I desperately wanted to understand my estranged daughter with the ultimate goal of persuading her to abandon this "Dad abused me" nonsense. But she had shut me out; I wasn't able to talk with her. Here before me was her figurative twin. This young adult likewise rattled off fabrications about her mother online, also declaring herself a victim of felony-level abuse, and she saw herself as a vindicator of her younger brothers and sisters. So went her narrative, almost a perfect mirror of my daughter's narrative of me. I wanted to run, but I also realized the incredible opportunity this was to crawl inside the head of a social smearer — someone who likewise unabashedly and unapologetically ravaged her parent's reputation online, just like my daughter — and understand how she saw the world.

"Do you mind if I sit down?" I asked. She consented.

What followed was an hour-long conversation about her hatred for her mother. She did virtually all of the talking. "I absolutely hate my mother," she insisted, followed with a litany of reasons justifying such a superlative emotion. I knew her mother, a former supporter of my business and the director of a debate tournament my children had attended in the past. I listened attentively to this young woman's seething hatred, seeing my daughter in her words and stories. I managed to ask a few probing questions, hardly able to get in a word or two, always trying to bring her back to *my* story. "You do realize that my daughter is not telling the truth, don't you?" I inquired.

"Don't you get it, Mr. Jeub?" she returned, as if I wasn't understanding that which was so obvious to her. *"The truth doesn't matter. Who cares what the truth is? She needs to tell her story, no matter what the truth is."*

This was the shell-shock bomb that triggers me to this day. The truth doesn't matter. I keep repeating it in my mind. The truth doesn't matter. The truth doesn't matter. *Really?* My daughter's online counterpart apparently was not going to be persuaded and was never going to waver from her support for my daughter, no matter what the truth was. I had thought that perhaps she and her friends might drop their affirmation for my daughter's online smearing once they knew of its deceit. But now I realized that was never going to happen. "Who cares what the truth is?" The narratives of online smearers, true or untrue, support one another. Like the warden and the guards in *The Shawshank Redemption,* the truth that could vindicate and free me from my prison was getting in the way of their greater agenda. My daughter's advocate would have none of it. *The truth doesn't matter.*

This was enlightening yet utterly demoralizing. I have always taught my students to seek the truth and to defend it. Yet here was my daughter's friend, just like my daughter herself, unapologetically advocating *untruth* for the sake of an emotionally personal "story" designed to ravage the lives of those with whom they held a grievance. Yet I also left awkwardly satisfied. This conversation helped me understand the sinister spell online smearers are under. Rational victims of smears — especially loving parents — naively believe that the truth will help mend their estranged relationships. It rarely does. Now that I understood how little objective, measurable, quantitative *truth* mattered in these online tirades, I likewise understood how little any *appeal* to that truth mattered. As a debate coach, I resolved to think of some higher level persuasion that I hadn't yet discovered, one that would convince my adversaries — even adversaries who are returning my love with hate — to abandon their coarse campaign.

The next month I attended a second national championship of a different debate league, which brought me back to my home state of Minnesota. I took the opportunity to reconnect with another friend from my high school years. The last connection we had was a year prior. He had just gone through a bitter divorce following his wife's extramarital affair. If that wasn't bad enough, his ex-wife made wild allegations about him being an abusive threat to their children. My friend fought the charges, persuading the court that there was no substance to them, and he eventually gained partial custody of his children. Even so, he suffered tremendous humiliation from the mere accusations brought against him, and the court battle was a drain to him financially as well as emotionally. You can see how I now related to my old friend, particularly from the unfair hatred my friend suffered during his divorce.

My friend had since gotten his life back together, rented an apartment close to the tournament I was attending, and had an extra room for me to stay in for the weekend. We talked late into our evenings together sharing our stories. He brought much hope back into my life when I witnessed how he had come through his version of public shaming. He was not a social media guy at all, living largely "off the grid" with no social presence to speak of. So I had to fill him in quite a bit on how that part of my world had caved in on me. He identified more than any of my other friends back home, even close family. "Guys like us are ripped to shreds," my friend empathized, "and no one seems to care what the truth is."

There was that strange new reality again: *the truth doesn't matter*. What's a guy to do with that? My friend had some answers that helped immensely. "I've learned a lot since my divorce, Jeuby," he said, using my high school nickname. "Looking back I realize that I pushed my wife away. I wasn't the best husband. If I knew then what I know now about how to treat a woman properly, she would have never cheated on me. My bitter divorce should have never happened, and I carry much of the blame."

As old friends do, I pushed back a bit. "Yeah, okay, maybe you were a bad husband. But you're no abuser," I said. "The truth is that she lied about you to gain custody of your children. That was wrong, it nearly ruined your life, and she should be ashamed of herself."

My friend smiled, as if knowing some deeper truth that I hadn't discovered yet. "Yeah, Jeuby, that attitude helped drive my wife away."

My friend then explained some specialized counseling he was receiving, tailored for men who had faced bitter divorces like his. Our conversation lasted late into the night, turning to my trials with my daughters. He listened intently, then asked a pointed question. "What is your relationship like with your sons?" I said they were great. I had only had trouble with my daughters, especially the three wrapped up in the online smearing. He then asked, "How did you treat your daughters when they flipped out?" I explained how I called them, emailed them, pleaded with them for counseling and reconciliation. He then offered me this judgment: "Jeuby, you don't know women like you think you do."

I resisted. I grew up with three sisters, and my wife loved me! My friend laughed. "No, you *think* you know women. You don't. I made the same stupid mistakes with my wife, turning her against me to the point that she tried to turn the courts against me, even our own kids away from their father. Truth is, that's evil, but that truth doesn't really matter when you're fighting for your life. I've learned a lot through my divorce. I think you have a lot to learn, too, Jeuby."

I was so desperately eager to understand my daughters, struggling to find my way through the mess I was in, that I was more open to rebuke than usual. I had to admit, the rational world of persuasion and debate — that which I was an expert in — meant nothing to my daughters nor the online court of public opinion. Remember, *the truth doesn't matter* to social smearers. I wondered if perhaps my friend had discovered some secret, advanced persuasion strategy that I hadn't yet figured out in my years of studying argumentation and debate.

"Tell me," my friend inquired again, seeming to know the focal point to discuss, "in more detail, how did you treat your oldest daughter when she started to rebel against you and the family?"

This brought back ancient history, way back to the TLC television days, eight years prior. There was no online smearing at the time. I'd simply term my oldest daughter as a *prodigal* — a biblical reference to the story of the Prodigal Son. She was secretly sneaking out and partying, and when we discovered it, her mother and I confronted her, just like parents should. I explained this to my friend: "I told her that she needed to repent of her sin and reconcile with her parents." My friend shook his head in disapproval. "Jeuby, Jeuby, Jeuby. You truly do *not* understand. The next time you see your daughter, you need to do the exact *opposite* of how you *think* you should act. If you want to win the hearts of your daughters, you need to start treating them like women, not men."

This was new advice for me, different than the "rational" ideas I'd been hearing from most friends and family, even different from what the professional counselor was saying to me back home. My friend reminded me that men had the innate desire to *fix*; women the desire to *feel*. In the heat of conflict, don't rationalize or persuade, as I naturally would in a tournament debate round. Instead, *charm* and *romanticize*. Make the moment magical, not logical. "Allurement is the skill to fulfill the opportunity," he told me, "not rectify a trauma." I remember arguing with my friend for a short while, explaining to him the logical problems my daughters had. "Chris, I understand that that's how you see it, but as badly as you want to straighten out that truth with your girls, you need to avoid it completely. Don't bring up the hard feelings or resentments at all. Ignore them." I held onto his words cautiously, but with extreme curiosity. He was challenging the way I processed the solutions to my problems. He encouraged me to consider a different approach to dealing with my daughters. "The next time you see one of your estranged daughters," he said, "open your arms and welcome them back, pretend the family trauma never existed, and have fun with them. You'll find that approach much more persuasive than your debate tactics."

My friend seemed to see a blindness in me, a blindness that is particularly typical in divorce situations. First, I needed to surrender my old sense of how effective (not how important) truth was to my daughters. Truth still mattered, but it didn't to my daughters, so my traditional, logical appeal to reasonable senses wouldn't work. Second, I needed to imagine the next encounter with one of my daughters — which would come sooner or later — and reconstruct how I would react. Judgment or condemnation would definitely backfire, but even an attempt — as much as I would have loved for it to happen — to return to the offensive social smearing and attempt to sort it out would backfire. I needed to ignore it altogether and try to, in the words of my friend, "have fun." Third, I needed to hide my desperation, my insistence to "solve" the problem. "Don't be so eager to fix it, Jeuby," he said. "Nothing will drive a woman away faster than your clumsy attempt to fix her." And he gave me a fourth strategy: Give them something insignificant but meaningful. "You will think it doesn't matter, that the truth of your situation matters more; but they will think the world of your gift and, ultimately, they will come around." My friend was convinced that this new strategy would, in fact, win my daughters back to the family. And the more we talked about it, the more I started believing the next opportunity to follow his advice would open doors rather than close them.

That chance came a month following my time in Minnesota with my friend. Another close friend, an assistant coach of a debate club I used to run, managed to get two tickets to see Rush, the classic Canadian rock trio, at the Pepsi Center in Denver for their 40th anniversary tour. Rush is perhaps the most famous band that *hardly ever* got played on the radio, considered the biggest "underground" band in rock history, and my friend and I were avid fans. I still owned vinyl records from the '70s and '80s. My friend knew of my trials, knew two of my daughters personally (he used to coach them for competitions) and knew I could use a break. So, we headed to Denver for an evening rendezvous with our rock 'n' roll past.

We walked the streets of Denver for a few hours before the concert, navigating through a flood of T-shirt wearing Rush fans. Hardly any of them were teenagers. The few we found were usually with their fathers. This evening seemed more of a family event than I expected, many fathers sharing the Rush experience of their youth with their teenage sons and daughters. This grew more and more depressing for me. You see, my daughter — the one who shared my gift in writing — also shared in my love for Rush, a nostalgia of my past when I was her age. If it wasn't for the social smear she participated in, chances were good that I would have been attending the concert with her, not my friend. Suddenly, attending the Rush concert became a stark reminder of my estrangement from my dear daughter, a smear nearly a year old now, and I had no idea at the time that it would have lasted so long. There was no one in the world I would have liked to enjoy the concert with more than her.

My friend sensed my rising sorrow, and I appreciated the way he expressed his sympathy. We were both debate coaches, so I told him about my high school friend's ideas of how to "persuade" my daughters back to the family. On an academic level, it was inherently interesting. The conversation lasted through dinner, our walk through Pepsi Center security, and all the way up to our third-level seats on the left side of the stage. We kicked back in our stadium chairs, still discussing my social media smear and how I planned to address my daughters when the next opportunity presented itself, waiting through those slow minutes before Neil, Alex and Geddy took the stage.

The stadium was getting close to being full when an audible, "Mr. Jeub!" was heard from the end of our row. It was the voice of a young lady, though the stadium lights were on behind her, and I was unable to make out who she was. "Sounds like one of your students," my friend said. I smiled in her direction, waved, and started the arduous process of walking over our seatmates — I was in seat number nine — to the aisle to greet whomever it was who called my name.

Shock. Confusion.

It was my daughter, my kindred Rush fan.

Her calling out "Mr. Jeub" is sort of an inside family joke. We traveled the country together running debate camps and attending tournaments. So in an environment full of other dads, I would mentally block out any shouts of "Dad!" even from my own children. A call of "Mr. Jeub!" was always rewarded with much greater success. And my kids always seemed to get a kick out of calling me "Mr. Jeub" to get my attention.

Can you imagine? Out of nearly 20,000 Rush fans at the Pepsi Center, my daughter's seat was about five rows behind mine. I had not seen her for nearly a year, and her online blogging of my alleged abuse continued. But here she was, smiling as if nothing bad had ever happened, stopping to say hi to her dad in Denver.

Allow me to ask you a question. How would you have acted in this situation? What would you have said? I will tell you how I would have responded before contemplating my old friend's advice. I would have frowned at her, making sure she knew I was hurt and troubled. Perhaps I would have even blurted out, "How dare you!" I would have jumped into debate mode, challenged her smearing narrative right there in front of Rush and everyone, reminding her of all the damage she had done to me, her family and the community from which she was raised.

I would have driven her further away, much further away than she already was, and likely rationalized my right to do so.

But this was my opportunity to do something different. I was coached and primed for it, so I made my move. "You look fantastic!" I said, ignoring our conflict altogether. "What have you been up to lately?" She told me she was working at a children's summer camp in the mountains. "Wow, that's great," and I followed with genuine praise, "you were always so good with children." I asked to give her a hug. She refused.

Pause.

Pain. Sadness.

I stammered out, "That's okay. I understand." Then, recovering, "It's just great to see you here. Wow, what are you doing here!?" I already knew the answer, "Dad, of course, *it's Rush*," she smiled. We laughed together. We agreed we wouldn't miss this concert for anything, and we laughed together more.

The conversation lasted only a scant minute or two. But it lasted for years. It was both surreal and shocking to us both, and I realized that she was waiting for my move. I can only imagine what was going through her mind, but I suspect she thought, "I wonder what Dad is going to say now?" I also hoped she was pleasantly surprised, because I once more applied my friend's pivotal coaching — to completely avoid the social smearing conflict and instead focus on what was important to her. I was aiming to form a bond, some sort of chemistry, and to connect quickly in the short opportunity I had. I was attempting a higher-level form of persuasion to reconnect with my beloved and estranged daughter.

After a bit more small talk, she closed the conversation. "Well, I guess I gotta go back to my seat." I didn't cling, nor did I appear desperate at all, something that I naturally would have, but would have likely killed the opportunity. "Yeah, I do, too." I said simply. "It sure is great to see you." I turned back to my seat. I wasn't yet done trying to connect with her, not even close! But I knew *she* needed to desire her return. It seems like a game, but it was what I had prepared to do, and I was putting all my hopes and dreams into its effectiveness.

"Holy wow!" my friend exclaimed, "that was your daughter!" He had been observing the entire thing, nine seats over, in awe. The concert hadn't yet started, and the two of us sat and wondered at the odds of such a meeting. Tens of thousands of Rush fans. Wow. Add in the fact that we had just been talking about my daughters and how I would respond if we met, and how we hoped for such an opportunity to come about. Holy wow, indeed.

I turned to see my daughter, five rows back. She was sitting by herself. I assumed she would be with friends, maybe from camp or from her social media community, but I saw her between two older people. She wasn't talking with them at all, so she appeared to be alone. My friend suggested that he switch seats with her, which was a great idea and would create another opportunity to connect. I again crawled over sitting people, exited my row and walked up to where she sat. "My friend offered to switch seats. Do you want to?" She hesitated. So I followed with her exact words: "Come on, *it's Rush!*"

She smiled and accepted my offer.

Rush is a unique rock band popularly known for its long concerts. This one lasted 3.5 hours with a full intermission, giving us a great amount of time to talk in between the songs. It was perhaps the perfect environment to begin winning my daughter back because it helped me to keep from going into our conflict. Trust me, I was tempted! But I held firm to my Minnesota friend's advice.

At one point I managed to shoot off a quick text to that friend, and he responded. "If you can buy her something, do it, something insignificant but meaningful." I decided on a T-shirt. When the concert ended, I reaffirmed how happy I was to see her and then offered to buy her a Rush shirt. This extended our time together as we left the stadium. I still doggedly refused to bring up our online discourse, and she avoided the subject as well. I bought two t-shirts and a poster, and, after we pulled the shirts on over our clothes, my friend took a photo of us together.

I wish I could testify that this single, amazing, even miraculous evening won my daughter over completely. But this story doesn't end so easily or perfectly. Still, I held it dear as a small step toward resolution. In the days that followed, she stopped her most malicious attacks, at least the attacks that were so vicious at the time. I consider this concert evening divinely orchestrated, and I refused to believe it would be the last time we connected. That night in the summer of 2015 temporarily brought two estranged people — a father and a daughter — back together to enjoy a nostalgic connection that was uniquely theirs. I still hope and pray that she turns completely away from her reckless online ways, but that's for her to do on her own. I know for certain now that I cannot persuade her in the traditional way. I let her go back to her life and respected the unspoken fact that she would not want me to post all over social media about our encounter. Instead, this is what I shared on Facebook:

> The Rush concert was amazing, as I got to spend an evening with the one person in the world I had wanted to spend it with most. It wasn't my carpool buddy, but an old acquaintance whom he graciously swapped seats with after we ran into each other at the concert. I hesitate to share with you who it was, but let's just say we grew up together with a like-minded love for this band. The night was definitely a Rush!

I shudder to think how I would have responded if I hadn't learned so much from my friend in Minnesota and my daughter's counterpart in South Carolina. I had been prepped and prepared for the smallest details of our conversation. Even the initial encounter, of smiling and waving to my daughter with the stadium lights blinding me behind her was a godsend. You can make the argument that she deserved to be chided, deserved to be persuaded, deserved to be shamed. But none of that would have accomplished that which I so deeply wanted, a relationship restored and renewed.

I hold a deep regret now that I had not known about this godly path to reconciliation back when I was dealing with my oldest daughter, the one I met when courting Wendy years ago, the one I adopted as my own. Her young-adult years were long past us, and the TLC show brought this conflict front and center when she faced rebuke and reprimand from her father, not patience and affection. I wish I could rewind time and recapture those moments. I had naively thought I was leading the family and being the loving dad. I had more to learn than I thought, though, and while the learning has been painful, it has caused me to be a much better parent today. It's amazing, isn't it? I'm a forensics coach, a professional who is paid to train others to be persuasive. But it was I who had just been taught octane-level persuasion, that which sways the unswayable, someone who hates you, to reconsider her ways and enjoy face-to-face time with the man she despises online.

Right before Andy Dufrensne breaks out of prison, he has an emotional conversation with his incarcerated comrade. By then everyone in Shawshank realizes Andy's innocence, but the warden refuses to call a retrial so that he can continue his own illegal deeds. Andy reflects on how he pushed his wife away, that he was perhaps the cause for her adulterous relationship, and that he deserved a life sentence in prison even though he didn't commit the murder.

I, too, often reflect on how I lacked tenderness toward my older daughters. But Andy truly was not a murderer, and I truly was not an abuser. He ultimately escaped his jail cell. I was still in my online prison. "Maybe you were a bad husband," Andy's friend replies, "but you were no murderer." My thoughts exactly.

Another opportunity has not opened up with my daughter since the Rush concert in Denver. I'm hoping for that time to come. When the time is right. When she is ready. I have, however, had that time with another daughter, one of the current bond of three smearers. It came later that year right around the one-year anniversary of the initial attack. That's another miraculous story that I will cover in the next chapter, one that helped break me from my prison.

My daughter and I after an evening of *Rush.*

Chapter 5: The Game

Those of us going through social smears feel like a mountain is crushing us. The losses we experience are immense, and when the smears come from people we know, especially from friends and family members we love, they seem to make the game unwinnable. And make no mistake: It is a game, a sport with players on the online field along with a mob of armchair quarterbacks making their judgments about whether we're being too soft or too hard, too lenient or too stubborn, too religious or having too little faith. When your reputation is being disparaged online, you are at the mercy of the internet society. You won't score any points by remaining silent, and it's an even bigger mistake to fight back, returning insults with facts, and thereby engaging the so-called trolls. I was a player locked in the walls of the labyrinth, searching for a way out, and when I played scenarios out in my head — counter-blogging, email campaigns, even litigation in court — all options seemed to lead to tearing my family further apart.

I wish online smearing was understood more, that it came with a handbook on etiquette, or had expected rules of engagement. It is more like guerrilla warfare than a civilized competition, a rapid ride down a chaotic wild river, never knowing what lies beyond the next twist in the stream. It became "the game" in my family's life as my daughters assailed me and the rest of my family — my wife, my other children, and sometimes even my extended family — while we tried to deal with the fallout. I desperately wanted to crack the nut of the social smearing world, just like I studied persuasive techniques and strategies of academic debaters. I reasoned, *there must be a way to win (or escape!) the game*, to persuade my daughters to leave their online hate behind, and to regain my family's reputation and online status. I was indeed "a gamer" with a brand new code to break, but I had no how-to manual at the ready.

My experience at the Rush concert — meeting up with my most adversarial daughter — was encouraging, but this game was far from over. My three daughters still held true to their online narrative that I was an abusive man who reigned with a hard heart and a heavy hand in his patriarchal home. The bitter pain from the recent past was still pounding, yet I took the Rush encounter as one little victory. The battlefield calmed down and the heat of war cooled for a time, allowing us much-needed breathing room to heal and bandage our emotional wounds. My entire family visited our counselor several times to help us sort things out. Those sessions didn't remove the online smear, of course, but they did help us begin to choose the right path for our lives and overcome the embarrassment of our situation.

I struggled most with my need to vindicate my family's name while still holding out hope for the children who were ravaging it. What a penurious dilemma I was in. My daily mood was unpredictable, to say the least. I felt incredible frustration at the injustice of my situation, then depression over any imagined attempt to deal with it. I was desperate for answers to help explain my situation and persuade my adversaries. But have you ever gotten into an online debate? Rarely does anyone "win." Remember, I'm a debate coach, a calculator of persuasion to win measured and strategic rounds at speech and debate tournaments. Yet I have found Facebook debates to be folly. No one ever wins, no one ever persuades anyone else, and the more you engage someone the more galvanized they become by their prejudiced beliefs, no matter how faulty or untrue. Thus, passionately engaging the social smearer is the Global Thermonuclear War of the social media world, and complete and utter destruction is no doubt the ultimate result.

Freedom from my social smearing would take *offline* experiences, not an *online* victory. Just as I did at the Rush concert, I needed to prepare to take full advantage of the next situation that presented itself. It was troubling and unjust to place my life at the whim of opportunity, but that's the kind of trench warfare I was in. I needed to figure out a way to win this war, or at least to claim a win for the Jeub family team. Thankfully, the next opportunity revealed itself sooner than I would have guessed, and it turned out to be a significant win that helped move the mountain that was crushing me and my family.

One of my sons — the one who suffered from extreme dyslexia — had quite the comedic run as a speech competitor. He helped fill our trophy shelf with top awards from tournaments all over the country, including five top titles, two for the same event in two different leagues, a record that has yet to be broken. I can take some credit for coaching him, but most of the credit goes to his intense study of comedy and speech technique. When he wanted to do a backflip as part of a presentation, he sought instruction from an Olympic gymnast; when he wanted to enter a creative interpretive event, he toured with a professional storyteller and comedian; and when he wanted to take comedy beyond high school competition, he joined an improv group in Colorado Springs.

As mentioned earlier, this son was arguably the most betrayed by his sisters. We were nearly an entire year into our family drama, and he had turned 18 over the summer, becoming my sixth adult child. Before the smear he had an incredibly close relationship with one of the "bond of three" sisters. She wasn't as much of a writer as my Rush-fan daughter, but she forwarded and reposted and "liked" the barrage of blog posts and follow-up comments that disparaged our family. My son at first challenged his sisters and attempted to debate with them in the blogosphere, but his sisters ridiculed him for his dyslexia-induced spelling errors. As I mentioned earlier in this book, they even began pointing to him as an example of "educational neglect" — yet another jab at my so-called abuse. My son was humiliated and embarrassed.

This made me so angry. My dyslexic son and destructive daughter used to be duo "interp" partners, performing a finalist rendition of *The Princess Bride*. I took them all over the country to perform the piece, and together they rose to 3rd place in the nation. It was an opportunity of a lifetime that few high schoolers ever get to experience. "Educational neglect," *whatever!* I was so upset with how this daughter now treated her brother as some sort of brainwashed subordinate who wasn't as "educated" as his older sisters. Do you ever find yourself fantasizing about the perfect rip to avenge yourself or your loved ones? I used to imagine chewing out my daughters, but my old high school friend was coaching me to resist the temptation to attack back, letting my innate anger toward injustice fall away. If I were to persuade my daughters to leave the online world of hate and social smearing, I'd have to win their hearts first. And I had to give up the idea of ever winning their minds. "You need to understand, Jeuby, that if you approach your daughters as the enemy, you will drive them further away," my friend instructed me. I had to love them in a way different than my instincts told me.

For social smearing that involves your family, "turning the other cheek" is a most difficult rule to follow. When someone posts an incriminating detail or gossips about a matter that should have remained private, the temptation to verbally rip into the guilty is intense. We may be able to remain calm and collected when strangers attack us. But loved ones? It's extremely difficult to keep your cool. It helps to focus on the end goal. I didn't need the satisfaction of unloading on anyone; I needed to reconcile the immediate family drama of three estranged daughters ruining my family and its reputation. I needed to plot my escape and redeem my family name.

I was working in my home office the morning of one of my son's improv events. We had plans to attend along with a few of the older kids. I had already been to one of his shows and — proud Dad moment — I thought my son was the funniest of the five comedians. We were looking forward to an evening of entertainment, but then he came downstairs to reveal disturbing news. He sat down in my opposing chair and dropped the headline: "My sister's coming to tonight's show," he said. "And she's bringing *some guy*."

Or maybe this *wasn't* so disturbing. Maybe another opportunity was availing itself. A couple of months had passed since my encounter with my other daughter at a Rush concert amid 20,000 other fans. Now another chance with another daughter was surfacing, this time at a small improv event with only a few dozen in the audience. Like I mentioned, the social smearing onslaught had ceased for the moment, and I liked to think it was because of that godsend Rush concert encounter, but I wasn't sure. My daughters had seemed to lose most of their childhood friends that they grew up with, and were now among new friends who identified with or at least shared in smearing. I could imagine that they were a lost bunch, letting the days roll by while holding bitterness toward their parents, making manufactured memories the basis for their online image. I didn't fully understand what was going on with the girls, and I certainly didn't know what the next move was in our relationship.

This brings to mind a mistake that many parents of estranged children — or *anybody* with an estranged relationship with *anyone* — tend to make. They believe their adversaries are perpetually in the same state of emotional estrangement as when the separation first occurred. This is seldom true. You should always keep in mind that your "enemy" may have come around to see the world differently, and you need to be open to the fact that they may be ready for reengaging. It shouldn't matter if the last encounter was a bitter fight or consisted of an irretrievable offense. If a spontaneous meetup presents itself, you should size up the situation and put your best foot forward.

For now, with my comedian son in my office explaining that my other daughter was about to "crash" his improv show that night — and she was dragging *some guy* with her — I had much to consider. How would *you* handle the situation? I knew I needed to take full advantage of the opportunity that presented itself, tuning my new persuasive technique up to optimal volume. I called my Minnesota friend to again seek his coaching, and he came up with a great plan. "Jeuby, don't make your daughter your focus tonight," he counseled. "Your focus should be *her guy.*"

Once more I thought this was odd advice, but my friend insisted on focusing on the guy, as if *he was* the target to hit. He said it would be an error to approach my daughter at all. This guy apparently had already earned her respect and admiration enough to bring him to her brother's show. Perhaps they were even getting serious by now. If I were to somehow convince him that I was a good guy and fellow advocate for my daughter's wellbeing, I would simultaneously succeed in convincing my daughter that I was a loving dad. In a debate round, it is equivalent to persuading your judge, not your opponent. Never mind your opponent; in the end it is the judge who fills out the ballot and declares you the winner.

"Do all you can to become best friends with your daughter's boyfriend," he coached me. "The temptation will be to turn to her, but you need to resist that. Ignore her. Let her observe you being the dad. It will feel like you're dissing her, punishing her even, and she might at first snap at you for doing so. Ignore any attempt by her to keep you from connecting with her boyfriend. Who knows, he may be a jerk, and perhaps he's a great guy, it doesn't matter. You will be the man in the room and you'll win your daughter's respect."

I was convinced, but I had a tough time convincing Wendy and the kids. Wendy admits today that, at the time, she wanted to do a little righteous-indignation yelling! Several of our children wanted to do the same, and my performing son — the most offended of all the siblings — wanted to at least tell her to stay home. I pleaded my case that we should do our best to take advantage of this opportunity to lead the "lost sheep" out of the madness she was in. The best way to do this was to love her where she was at as if the conflict didn't exist, trying our best to get to know her boyfriend. Any other plan would lead to disappointment, I argued, perhaps even to further conflict that we would all regret.

The improv show was at a small art studio downtown. Wendy and I were seated already when our daughter and her boyfriend came in. I wasted no time. I left my seat and rocketed straight toward them, put my hand out to *the guy* and said, "Hi! I'm Chris."

Of course he shook my hand. "Hey," he said, smiling, introducing himself to me.

"I'm super-glad you could make it tonight to see my son perform," I told him. "Did you know my son has been really enjoying improv? He was a champion speaker, and he and his sister were duo partners back in the day. Had she ever told you so?"

And so went the chitchat. I barely looked at my daughter. My full focus was on *the guy*. I led him away from my daughter to introduce him to Wendy, and she, too, made him the center of attention. By now the siblings were talking with our "lost sheep," allowing Wendy and I to become friends with her guy. It turned out, thankfully, that he was a very kind, intelligent and insightful man. There was not too much ice to break through after all. In that 10 minutes prior to the show, my daughter's boyfriend and I had fun conversing, and I had barely said a word to my daughter.

The show lifted the spirits of everyone in the audience. My son and the other improv performers lit up the place with bellyaching laughter. I continued to give my daughter's boyfriend all of my attention after the show, getting to know him the best I could. I learned that he was trained in massage therapy. I told him that I had a kink in my neck, and he immediately shot into therapy mode, asking me to do all sorts of twists with my arm as he massaged my neck. He gave a small stand-up massage to Wendy, too. I like to think he felt welcomed by my family, with nary a single judgmental or skeptical glare coming from any of us in the Jeub family — *as if there was no family drama at all.*

My friend back home in Minnesota would have been proud. Because this was the point. I largely ignored my daughter, and I totally ignored any of her past injustices toward the family. We left the improv that night liking her boyfriend — sincerely, we were not being fake; he appeared to be a great guy — and I was eager to see him again. I gathered that he felt the same. We left for home, and they left for theirs, wherever that was. We hadn't made that a point of discussion at all. We enjoyed the evening together, getting to know one another and having a great time. I bet my daughter's *guy* lit up a conversation with her that began something like, "So, what's so bad about your dad again?" After which my daughter probably began to reflect, *I'm not sure.*

Pause again now and consider how you would have handled the situation — or, at least, what conventional wisdom would have called for. My daughter had been one of the three girls who had done us great damage, and we had no reason to believe that she had changed at all. We had every right to take that biblically figurative eye for an eye, tooth for a tooth, and lay into her for her offenses. But desperate times call for desperate measures, and when you consider the effectiveness of my friend's advice, it convinces you to reconsider. At the start of the evening my daughter had been an avowed adversary to my family name, and I suspected her boyfriend was an enabler. Appeals to civilized conversation, confrontation, logic or reason, or any other conventional attempt to bridge the gap of our relationship would have been futile — folly, no doubt, much like a Facebook debate — surely backfiring and leading to a more disastrous void. Instead, by the end of the night my daughter seemed to be reconsidering her adversarial stance, which was exactly where she needed to be. There would be no winning my online "game" without her being in a repentant, ready-to-reconcile frame of mind, but I needed to change my own attitude and approach in order to lead her there. *It worked like a charm!* And "charm" it certainly was, even netting me a neck massage from *her guy.*

"Facing hate" is perhaps one of the most brutal and unjust conflicts a person can be in. Any parent with a prodigal son or daughter — whether or not they are socially smeared online — understands the dire straits this situation is. The hater cares nothing for you, but you care deeply for the hater. In every way the smearer is your enemy — they want you humiliated and ruined — yet, when they are part of your family, you want them reconciled and back to their functional selves. Ignoring the trial altogether and reaching out to the one who made your life so difficult is, in itself, one of the most difficult things you will attempt to do. But that is what truly converts someone. It's not about *beating* your enemies. It's about *loving* them.

This daughter was the youngest of the three sisters still holding onto the online narrative of abuse, and she wasn't yet free from the knotted bond. The offenses against our family were difficult to forget. We remembered this particular daughter as the "stalker." She didn't write much online — sharing and liking her sister's writings were more her style — but she did the most to try to lure other children at home into their bond. During one of our out-of-town trips the year before, she sneaked into our home and left gifts and notes for her siblings, leaving her cell number in case they, too, wanted to "escape." She showed up at our children's school — the local charter school that six kids attended — making the school's vice principal think it as a security breach. I had to then fill him in to the social media smear we were dealing with. So my daughter had the appearance of being predatory, and our distrust in her ran pretty high.

Herein lies one of the most difficult realities of the modern dilemma of online smears. They do incredible, lasting damage to relationships. It is not at all like an impassioned shouting match in the privacy of your home where both participants can say sorry and make up. In our case our daughters had *thousands* of viral strangers to fess up to, while Wendy and I had thousands more who wanted explanations. We all had the judgment of the various online mobs to counter, and the humiliation of the exposure of our family drama to the online world to consider. It was nearly impossible for us to simply "forgive and forget," just as it was unfathomable to think our "stalking" daughter would fess up to fabricating the narrative of our so-called dysfunctional family. This was surely going to be a difficult journey out of the social smearing mess.

I recall the months before the blog-post bombs started dropping. This particular daughter had moved out to live with her older blog-writing sister — the two just two years apart in age — in a basement apartment close to college. The two began taking jabs at Wendy and me in private, accusing us of the very vices that eventually were articulated online for the world to read. I still remember weathering the biting conversations with much hope, listening to their grievances and trying hard to understand their pain. We carried on, just like my parents did in my youth, quietly taking the news of our children's reimagined upbringing. It was together that the two first made the accusation that we abused them. We suggested that we all see a counselor for help. We believed at the time these were some sort of manufactured memories, something much deeper than simple conversations could resolve. We denied their claims of abuse, and they insisted we were lying, and that is how the conversation halted our relationship.

At first the girls agreed to counseling, but they insisted the counselor be a "professional" counselor (not a pastor or respected friend of the family) and that we pay for it. At least this was better than a flat refusal, so we agreed and found a Ph.D. in Colorado Springs who agreed to meet with us. The first session was a meeting with Wendy and me. We had scheduled a second session where the girls would meet with the counselor privately, the plan being we would meet together for a third session and try to reconcile. This was the agreed plan between all of us, and our daughters were set to meet with the psychologist in October 2014. You now know the route the girls took from there. Our hope for reconciliation was crushed when the girls went on their social smearing rampage — and their oldest sister, the third in the "bond of sisters," joined in. They never did meet with the counselor.

I believe that if they had chosen counseling, so much pain could have been avoided. For them, as well as the rest of the family. Rather than weeks or even months of counseling and reconciliation, we got public fighting and smearing that went on for years. The first month of the public smear was the most devastating for our family, but even then we held out hope. Recall the reaching out I did weeks into the smear — inviting them to the birthday party of our twins. We wanted reconciliation so badly, wanted to try to understand their rage and hatred, and if a simple birthday party would help move closer to that, then we would move heaven and earth to make sure the sisters could come. "Not interested," she coldly replied.

This was who we remembered, truly a prodigal daughter, one who left home in a huff and made sure we didn't follow. The metaphorical prodigal — represented in the book of Luke in the Bible — eventually repents, returns to his father, begs for forgiveness for sinning against him and against God. It is a mistake for parents to imagine this glorious return of their wayward children, for it rarely happens all at once with pomp and circumstance. I have found that prodigals return in small steps, little by little, one concession at a time. Parents need to be very careful not to upset this incremental process and lose more ground than they gain, making reconciliation more difficult as time goes on. Whip up a social smear involving countless online strangers on social media, and you'll see just how hard the mountain is to move.

I drove home the night of the improv feeling extremely optimistic, more so than I had in a year. I felt incredibly empowered with my newly discovered persuasion powers. This was a breakthrough for me! I had finally found a method to solve the mad stalemate that plagued my family. These attempts to persuade and influence were different than the logic and reasoning methods I taught in my life's work as a debate teacher. In traditional debate, your opponent agrees to follow the rules; in a social smear, you're dealing with chaos and lawlessness.

These new strategies were miraculously effective twice in a row — the first at the Rush concert, the second at the improv — and I followed both with simple gifts of affection. Just as I bought my blogging daughter a T-shirt at the Rush concert, I ordered a coffee mug and coffee and had them delivered to my "stalking" daughter. She responded with appreciation. The goal of opening up communication with her had succeeded far beyond any "logic and reasoning" email exchange or shouting match would have brought. The method (which more precisely could be called my change of heart) was working, and I was eager to keep applying the techniques. So I added a note to the gift that kindly asked her to follow through with the counselor we originally scheduled the year before.

My family was still skeptical. My daughter's teenage sisters, especially, had difficulty forgetting her predatory behavior the year before. Remember how my other adult children were solicited to join the smear? The same attempts to sever them from the family were made with our teenage girls, and the so-called "stalker" was the most aggressive, even one time trying to influence them to run away from home. Wendy, too, had doubts about how repentant she was now, afraid that perhaps this was just another attempt to "rescue" her siblings from their "abusive" home. I was optimistic, but the rest of the family was suspicious.

At first I accused them of being paranoid. This was finally our chance to welcome in the prodigal child, "kill the fattened calf" and celebrate reconciliation! Our family needed a victory, and I didn't want this ship to pass. Wendy and I had a sharp disagreement about how to reach out to our daughter. I wanted to seek her out, as if I were the shepherd seeking out his lost lamb. Wendy suspected a trap, another attempt from her daughter to wreak havoc in our lives. I wanted another chance to guide her back into the family; Wendy wanted to protect the family we had left.

That's where the argument hung, so I called my friend, expecting him to agree with me. "No, Jeuby," he said. "Listen to Wendy. She's absolutely right." He then started to push me toward another higher-level idea, encouraging me to play it cool and avoid appearing desperate or foolish. He urged me to wait. "The coffee gift was perfect because it keeps her thinking of you whenever she uses it," he coached me, "but the request for counseling was clumsy. It showed desperation and weakness. You have to wait it out, respect her time, and let her truly come back to you." He continued: "And listen to Wendy! She's a deep woman with intuition that surpasses yours. You can't treat women like men, Jeuby. That's your problem. Wendy knows this: She can see your eagerness to fix the situation, but she sees it as weakness. You will only push your daughter away, maybe even Wendy, too, just like I did with my wife. Remember, they need to *feel* it, so you need to wait."

I took the reprimand, feeling a bit "schooled" by my friend, but I now see he was absolutely right. My daughter accepted her coffee gift, but she pushed against my request for counseling. "I feel I am not ready," she emailed. I tried to recover and keep my cool, responding that it was fine. "In your own time," I replied. Nearly four weeks followed before she responded again. It was October 2015, a full year into our social smear, when my daughter finally began seeking restoration with her family. The four weeks of "stewing" over our predicament allowed for all of us to consider the situation. And it was a very busy month. My Australia-residing daughter and her Syrian husband flew into the States for the celebration of my parents' 50th wedding anniversary. They stayed the entire month of October, traveled America (my son-in-law had never been to the U.S.), and we spent much time in deep discussions of our family ordeal.

These were painful weeks for me. Sure, it was great that my daughter visited from Australia and my parents celebrated 50 years of marriage, but my tarnished online reputation was seriously hurting my business. Summer camp attendance dropped by more than half (would you send your kid to summer camp when its leader was publicly accused of abuse?), and sales of my resources took a hit, too. My manly need to fix the public smear swelled inside me, though I still submitted to Wendy's intuitive resistance, suppressing my fighting spirit. The result? I found myself depressed over my lack of options. Waiting is very difficult. I hated admitting it, but this is exactly what the biblical father of the prodigal son did. He didn't go out into the mucky world to drag his boy back. He stayed home with the rest of the family and waited for his lost son to return. I'll bet it was very difficult to do so.

Those of us who are estranged from loved ones must realize that time doesn't stand as still as we think. I discovered later that my daughter was, in a way, being coached by *the guy* she brought to the improv. Unbeknownst to any of us, he was working on my daughter's perception of her family. He came from a troubled family of divorce and abuse that *really* happened. When my daughter would divulge the details of her supposed abuse, her boyfriend would reply, "That's it?" My daughter would try to explain how bad her parents were, and he would counter, "Let me tell you about *my* parents." For these four weeks of me "waiting" for something to happen, my daughter's *guy* was working hard to get her to see that her parents weren't that bad at all.

To me it seemed like an eternity, but my daughter did finally contact me. She requested a meeting with the family. I didn't want to make the same sloppy mistake of appearing desperate, so I said, "No, we're not ready." I explained that I, personally, was fine with a meeting, but the rest of the family was not. This wasn't untrue, but it had more to do with applying the advice that my friend laid out for me. It made me appear the defender of my daughter, as if I was the pathway to reconnecting with her family, which is exactly what she would respond best to. As a compromise, I offered the idea of going to coffee with just Wendy and me — and her older sister (still in town from Australia) with her husband. An agreement was made, and we set up a time to meet.

We had only met my daughter's *guy* once. We liked his carefree spirit, but we had no idea how much of a positive influence he was. By this time we had discovered they were living together somewhere in the mountains, but not much more than that. A younger Chris Jeub would have jumped to all sorts of conclusions, followed quickly with the worst pronouncements of judgment. But by then I felt I had no grounds to judge anyone, so I accepted their relationship for what it was. In a spiritual way, I was letting God sort out the lifestyle of my adult child, and I have found this to be a much more successful approach with all of my children. They know my views and they know how they were raised, but their questionable life choices as adults are for them to deal with. I only deal with problem behaviors when they conflict with my life directly, and them living together was far from my current conflict.

Besides, I could tell something was changing in my daughter. A few emails were exchanged to set up the coffee date, and she would close her notes with "In Agape love" and "I love you Dad!" This was new. If I were to halt that kind of progress just to stick my fatherly nose into her adult business, I would have senselessly destroyed everything. I have come to understand that when we as parents insist on condemning our children for the adult lifestyles they have chosen, all we do is wall them off, sometimes forever. When they are adults and you have been cast out of their lives, you need to hold your judgment and — as painful as it is — wait.

My Syrian son-in-law was changing me, too. He was a citizen of Australia, but he grew up in Aleppo, his home now destroyed by the civil war. His parents were refugees in Turkey where he married my daughter. I had already spent two weeks with him six months prior in Australia, but this time he was in my home and I had gone through so much since then. I had learned just how much influence he had on my daughter when she was struggling with me. She, as you already know, also professed a childhood of abuse, but my son-in-law counseled her to still respect her parents and love them. He was raised in Syria, and he insisted that mild punishment in his Muslim community would look like severe abuse in America, so, like my other daughter's *guy*, he counseled her to appreciate her parents more.

We met at a local coffee shop. Three women (Wendy and our daughters) and three men (me and my daughters' *guys*). We were all tense, expecting perhaps a raging argument about the past. Who knew what was going to happen? We were all playing a game, not able to predict the next move. We greeted one another cordially enough, the girls went to the counter to buy a round of coffees, and the guys gravitated to the elongated booth in the corner of the shop. My daughter's boyfriend sat on one side, my son-in-law and I on the other. The massage-therapy pro jumped right in, and what he said was surprising. Paraphrased:

> "OK, guys. I am doing everything I can to bring my girlfriend back to her family, but it has been very difficult. Chris, she shares nothing but the best stories of your family, but she seems to think she was abused and neglected. I don't really care how much of it is true. I know that she misses her mom and siblings, and we need to get her to wise up and respect you and return to her family. I need your help to convince her, guys. I think she's ready."

The two of us sat and listened, jaws slightly agape. We hadn't known how much of an advocate this man had been. The girls arrived with our coffees, and together the six of us remained in our seats for two hours, Wendy and her daughter doing virtually all of the talking. This was where the conflict and tension remained. My daughter expressed how she wanted to see her siblings, but Wendy countered with her reasonable suspicions. My daughter said she had changed her mind a lot since knowing her boyfriend. Wendy expressed how much pain she had caused the family. My daughter shared her desire to reunite with her siblings. Wendy explained how she felt so betrayed by her daughter's actions the year before. Many tears were shed at that table, and the rest of us spent much of our time quietly listening to the exchange between mother and daughter. We left the conversation satisfied, vowing to bring news of the meeting back to the siblings.

The few words I spoke into the conversation were affirmations of what I had already told my daughter: I was personally fine with her reconnecting with the family, but the rest had reservations. This showed her my willingness to protect her from embarrassment or counterattack. My heart was eager to reconcile her with the family she smeared, but my flesh often clawed at me to meditate on the injustice of it all. My friend wisely counseled me to bury my feelings and stay focused on the goal. "Your daughter is just like any daughter: they have the innate need for their father's protection," he said. "You have many daughters, but you can protect all of them from one another. Let this play out, Jeuby. You can do this!"

I had doubts about the arranged sibling meeting. The young ones weren't a part of it, but the older teens were, and we met at a restaurant in Colorado Springs. It went better than I thought it would. Almost immediately the old laughs between siblings lit up the restaurant. Jokes flew from sibling to sibling, many of the sentences started by one being finished by another, and the joy of a happy family kept the place hopping. Sibling bonds are arguably the strongest bond in family life, even stronger than a parent-child bond. It was as if there was no history of a social smear at all. I sat and mostly observed the reconciliation of the lost prodigal with her siblings. It was beautiful.

My daughter and her boyfriend visited several times that winter. I insisted they sleep in separate rooms, an expectation in my home that they never challenged. None of our reconciliation was displayed to the online world, and by then this daughter had largely shut down her social media altogether. Still, the online smear was being pushed away from our current life, and that was very, very nice! My daughter's boyfriend and I started to become friends. He asked for my blessing, I gave it, and he proposed to my daughter. A year later we climbed to 12,500 feet for their wedding held at the tree-line on a Colorado 14er beside a majestic lake. All of the Jeub children — all but our Australian daughter and the two remaining sisters still holding onto the online narrative of our abusive family — made the seven-mile hike to join in the celebration. Wendy and I walked our daughter up a wooded trail leading to the top of a lakeside boulder, and I handed her over to *her guy*.

We did more than just climb a mountain that day. *We moved it.* This was a significant victory in rebuilding our family's reputation and bringing our daughters — the strand of three cords "not easily broken," as the Bible says — back into the family. Isn't it interesting how the *offline* relationship began to take apart the *online* narrative and show the greater truth? The Jeub family is a huge family full of love and empathy, not an abuse-ridden home of crazy haters. The tide of this social-smearing war started to turn toward us. I began winning the online game by leaving it.

Most of the Jeubs committed to the 14-mile roundtrip hike up the mountain to attend the marriage of one of my prodigal daughters. We began to see how mountains truly *can* be moved.

Chapter 6: Heart Rock

Domestic abuse victims often take photos of the truth: burns, scars, bruises, etc. Photos are indicting, and they become strong evidence in convicting abusers of their crime. But where there is no crime, there can be no photo. And, indeed, there was no photo to help the online world validate the initial claim that the Jeub family was the "house of horror" the tabloids wrote about. Still, for some, the claim alone was validation enough to make their judgment against us. I realize today that much of my defense was relevant only to the rational and civil-minded, those seeking the truth of the matter. But I had learned, from the lips of my daughter's friend, that for so many in her online generation, "the truth doesn't matter." Thus, the online world left little to be salvaged for the accused abuser.

What is this thing you call "truth"? This is the online mob's presumptive question of which it cares little for an answer. If someone presumes no measurable, objective truth by which to live, that person is free to live by his or her own created "truth." To any problem that presents itself, any predicament that arises, any question asked about life, the answer for the mob is, "Whatever." No evidence is needed, no further research necessary. The end justifies the means, so smearing another human being regardless of the truth is perfectly justified to the collective judgment of the mob.

This is the antithesis of academic debate, at least how I have taught it for two-and-a-half decades. I entered the activity in 1995 and found it to be the perfect truth-seeking activity I craved as a young teacher. Debate is the educational activity of placing two opponents against each other in a controlled arena of competition, both to argue the two sides of a proposition. I taught my daughters how to think strategically through the most controversial policy and value debates, to seek corroboration for their claims, to anticipate cross-examination of their ideas and answer confidently.

Much of the smear that I faced online portrayed me as a legalistic, dogmatic dad, a "my way or the highway" kind of jerk who had little patience for anything other than my own judgments. Every aspect of my teaching — years of curriculum development and study of debate technique — taught the exact *opposite* of the online narrative from my adversaries. Understand how debaters come to the truth: Faced with a proposition, they hold their opinion and first let their research guide them. Second, they formulate claims with the evidence and expert guidance (not their own) forming strong validation for any contention they propose for their case. And, third, they anticipate opposing arguments, rationally address them while developing well-rounded responses to help convince the judge. Even after all this analysis and justification for the sake of truth, they hold themselves open to correction, further research and alternative views that will help modify or strengthen their position. In a sentence, *debaters are the kindest, most open-minded, most nonjudgmental people I know.*

Social smearers are the exact opposite. They turn the rational process of debate on its head. Claims are made before any research is gathered, and research is seldom required at all. Accusations are made early in the process of truth seeking, as few care for the truth anyway. If the claims are not fabricated altogether, they are purposely exaggerated in order to shock the judge into condemnation of the defendant. The claim is usually so vile that the judge — in social media, this is the mob of strangers watching from their elevated social media platforms — will seek no validation for the claim. Any attempt at defense is beaten down and shamed.

Social smearers are not debaters at all, then. They are bullies.

It took me a long time to understand that I was not able to change the archenemy of my debate theory, even when they were my own daughters. Worse yet, I had to come to terms with the fact that my daughters — trained in persuasive strategy — knew their audience better than the average "truth is relative" millennial. They easily persuaded the gullible mob to go along with their enticements, like ignorant, emotional rubes whipped up to use their keyboards and phones as pitchforks and torches. My daughters knew the questions before they were asked, and they leveraged the online world to make sure their smear was as damaging as possible. I was banned from convincing anyone online that I was innocent of the charges, for the measurement of my guilt or innocence was not the truth, as all crime should be. The mob was my judge and jury. There was no winning in this kangaroo court.

It doesn't help my situation much, but I find some solace that I am not the first victim of angry mobs. I think of Tom Robinson in *To Kill a Mockingbird*, the fictional account of a black man convicted of rape in the 1930s. His defense was reasonable and convincing, but the town mob overwhelmed the righteous path and, instead of acquitting him, killed him. And there's no doubt that this story resembled many other lynchings throughout history. The Salem Witch Trials of the 17th century were rigged affairs that left no option of a genuine defense to the accused, torturing them until a "confession" was made and they either died from the torture or were sentenced to death after their confession. Strange, isn't it? They used an awful, barbaric method of torture to "find the truth," but it was no truth at all. The crucifixion of Jesus Christ likewise came about when a mob overrode Pontius Pilate's assertions of his innocence. Study this passage (John 18:28-40) and you see stark similarities to social smearing. Pilate advocated for Jesus' freedom, but he relented to the angry mob calling for his crucifixion. "What is truth?" the governor inquired of Jesus. But he didn't wait for a response, instead pressing on, sentencing our Savior to death.

These days, we metaphorically refer to unjust trials as "modern-day lynchings," "witch hunts" and "crucifixions." In all of these examples, the truth was relative, a preconceived conclusion that justified the hanging, torture or lashings that preceded the inevitable deaths. Debaters never believe claims that are not duly briefed and researched, and they are taught to resist the fallacious appeal to sympathy from the most egregious claims. Conversely, our brave new world of social media participants are arrogant and unjust, quick to judge, gleeful ruiners of reputations without any inquiry or investigation. They surrender to their primal instincts. They let their hate guide them.

The online world we live in today can be awful. It can be a hell on earth. The socially smeared are hanging from nooses, burning at the stake and hanging on crosses along the horizon of the internet. Is there any freedom from this injustice? There is, but for me there was first a valley of death that I had to traverse. It left my heart most heavy, like a rock.

The successes of my recent past with two of my daughters caused me to reach out to my oldest daughter, the one who was the central focus of our TLC show nearly a decade prior to our social smear. She was now living with a man and had two other children with him — all three of whom we were forbidden to see. I attempted to approach the young dad as I had approached the other men in my daughters' lives. I hoped he would be much like the others, eager to have my daughter reconcile with her parents and perhaps return to the semblance of a loving family. Instead, he declined any of my attempts to connect, and my hopes were crushed.

All of my daughters, by this time, had mostly puttered out from lambasting their family with fabrications of childhood abuse, which was good. This oldest one retreated to her boyfriend and his family, buying a home and applying her skills to a career that brought them modest wealth. The other shifted her blogging to bizarre, experimental writings of spiritual prophecy, mental illness, and leftist activism. I couldn't bear to keep up with them. It is extremely painful to see a gifted child walk away from the foundations of their upbringing. Even more troubling was seeing how many people followed her down her dark and dreary path. Many would encourage her, call her "brave" and "fearless," and even support her financially through her Patreon campaign that claimed she was working on a book that would further expose her family of all sorts of fallacious crimes. Some even followed her down the path of posting whatever stories in their own pasts they could come up with to socially shame their own parents. It pained me to see my daughter's writing skills — no doubt her persuasive debate powers that I raised her with — being used to promote debauchery and hatred.

This was the darkest valley of my life. Few people have understood the depression I faced. Our family psychologist — as well as my sister, a school counselor with a master's degree in psychology — suggested I struggled with symptoms similar to Post-Traumatic Stress Disorder. Both had professional experience with PTSD, particularly dealing with war veterans. When a war veteran — who has experienced horrors far beyond what they expected — returns to civilian life, friends and family want to know what it was like. But the veteran doesn't want to explain it. Even when he does try to explain it, it never compares to the actual experience, an experience the veteran didn't want to explain to anyone in the first place. This leads others to misjudge and misunderstand, but the veteran just wants to return to his pre-war self. It's a stress that follows the trauma; the veteran cannot solve it, and we call the symptoms of all this PTSD. It is a dark and lonely journey.

Trauma is also common for the socially smeared. No one really understands it until it happens to you. The weight of a social smear — the embarrassment, the injustice, the cruelty you face, the paranoia that sets in — is the most traumatic ordeal I have ever experienced. It was like I was stripped naked and lashed in the public square, surrounded by jeering judgment and ridicule from the gathering mob. And though I had returned to civilization and restored many of my relationships in the aftermath, I had trouble explaining to anyone the suffering that I withstood. People tried to encourage me, but no encouragement lifted me from my depression. And the more I tried to explain myself, the more hopeless I got about my situation. It truly was a disorderly stress following a significant trauma.

I remember feeling like no one understood me, even my closest friends and family members. Friends would ask how I was doing, and I would smile and mouth an "OK" or a "fine," but secretly I would be thinking, "I don't even want to begin to explain how awful I feel." It would do no good; they wouldn't understand. My children — the older ones still at home — moved on emotionally and socially within a year or two. They would ask me why I still held onto the past, resilient as they were. Even Wendy grew impatient with me and my depression, feeling that I should let go of the trial and move on with life. So on April 13, 2017, I attempted to explain to my family what I was still going through. I penned this letter, a letter I never sent:

> *Dear Family,*
>
> *It has been more than two years since my daughters began their brazen attacks against our family. They used every tool they could muster to bring us ruin. I would like to say that they failed, but I need to humbly offer that they succeeded. I can't win this fight. I am in ruin.*
>
> *I struggle nearly every day with depression. A weight of despair haunts me. The smallest task at hand becomes a difficulty. Sometimes my knees buckle and I lie in bed. My humor leaves, I sigh heavily, and I frown often. People try to remind me of my many blessings, but I do not believe them. Instead, I wallow.*
>
> *I struggle with work. I was once a teacher, an educational cheerleader, an enthusiastic evangelizer for debate. I had many great people supporting me and my work. Some have tried to continue at my side, but all have kept a comfortable distance. No one really backs me, for I remain accused of heinous crimes against innocent children. And because I have refused the debate, they ask, "What does he have to hide?" I'm deemed guilty without a defense.*
>
> *I struggle trusting anyone. I do not trust that my children will grow in truth and greatness. They will likely turn on me and on God, perhaps join my prodigal children, when they are tempted to take up their story. Distant relatives were not supportive. Closer ones were, or at least they thought they were. At best they believed me and felt bad for my trials, but no one stood up and called out my adult children.*
>
> *In their own way, everyone believes they were supportive. Even people who sympathized with [my daughter] believed that they were being helpful. Those who directly betrayed me—past friends and family cousins—had some twisted idea that they were helping my family. They prejudged this problem to*

be my problem, somehow the end-result of my fathering — too strict, too conservative, too religious, too much into debate. They wanted me to fess up and accept my penance, my punishment, my pain. I somehow deserved it, and denial would only prolong my suffering.

I guess my punishment is trying to raise a home in God's love. Peace, love in God and one another, goodness for all. In a way, this is my prayer: God's Kingdom, on earth as it is in heaven. But no one believes me. They think I am pretending, that I am the fabricator of lies and my children's deceit is a byproduct of my deception. In their judgment, I am a mastermind and Great Deceiver, someone who spins his lies to control others and wield power.

This is the reason for my great sadness. I have been targeted — successfully — to be killed and destroyed. My flaw was not in my intention to build peace, love and goodness for this world. It was in my desire to build these values the best I could in my corner of worldly influence. I was doing a pretty good job. And I looked forward to sharing in the prosperity with others through my ministry, my work, and my family.

The Resistance made sure that it would not spread, even to my own children and family. My sadness is as real and consistent as the morning. This is my war. And I have lost it.

Wendy found my computer open to this letter, and her response was not pleasant. We had drifted apart and, like I shared, she was growing irritated with my depression. We have different perspectives of how this happened, and let me first explain how she saw it. She saw depression as a weakness, a surrender to the fight that I should have been participating in more heartily. Wendy would say to me often that I should forget my daughters, focus instead on my many other children, get on with life, and ignore the social smear. I was misinterpreting my ordeal, letting it ravage our lives rather than overcoming it. She believed I was feeding my depression, and this led to an emotional spiral downward that caused many of our family problems. The rest of my children needed a dad, my business needed an executive, and my wife wanted back the man she married. Indeed, I was not the man I used to be. And my wife felt that she had been more than patient with me, for quite long enough.

Did it matter if I was offended by this? I felt that Wendy was quite cruel to me at this depressing time in my life. Years prior when the twins were born, Wendy suffered from anxiety attacks. I was 100% supportive, all-in with the task of keeping Wendy protected during this vulnerable time. That fact made it all the more easy for me to feel now like she was dropping me cold when I went through a similar anxiety, mine in the form of depression. I had wanted to fight online, but Wendy thought it served no purpose, so I felt my fighting spirit being suppressed, like a warrior whose wife begs for him to stay home from battle. I saw ignoring the social smear as putting blinders on, giving up, not *fighting!* This idea spiraled me further into depression, giving Wendy more reason to blame me for our stress, and matters compounded as time rolled on.

I will never forget the fight we got into in the driveway, remaining in our car to hide our shouting match from the children. I had suggested Wendy get a job to help with our financial struggles, and she tried to convince me that that was quite impossible. Our schedules, skills and ideals were built around me being the breadwinner, she being the runner of our children's activities. I could not see a break in my finances, and she could not see a break in her duties either. She continued to blame me for the problem, and I pressed for her to help out more. Wendy saw herself as giving me a kick back to reality, and I saw her as resisting work that would help alleviate our financial stress.

You, dear reader, are right now probably judging me or my wife. You either agree with Wendy that I should get off my duff and get back to work, or you agree with me that Wendy should put in her fair share and quit depending on me so much. Can you see how we were headed for disaster? I used to easily judge couples who would divorce following a family trauma. A child dies, a teen rebels, a bankruptcy is suffered. "I guess it shows troubles were going on already," I would quip. But I get it now. Circumstances do lead to failures, and shame on me for ever assessing failure as merely a sign of underlying troubles. My own case in point: The social smear from my daughters nearly ruined our marriage, and it had not one thing to do with troubles that were already there.

This was so different from the way we used to be. Wendy and I started our marriage with rock-solid counsel and direction. We would pray every night together, committing to each other in all we set out to do. We walked together in unison through all of life's trials. I believe we once had the best marriage in the world. Now, sitting in the car being reprimanded like a child, I felt like calling it quits. Wendy was so seething angry, she considered the same. For the first time in our marriage, we both saw divorce as a viable option. This was the lowest moment of our life together.

I'm glad to say that we didn't give the devil his due in this regard. Here's how we battled the infernal temptation: We hiked. We live a mile away from Colorado's largest woods, the million-acre Pike National Forest. Mt. Herman overlooks our little town of Monument like a mound of greatness, offering miles of trails to pack into. Wendy and I now had our own mountain to move, that of our marriage. We refused to justify a separation. Instead, we packed our backpacks with lunchmeat, deli cheese and a bottle of red wine. We proceeded to spend several afternoons in the mountains of Monument.

Therapy is expensive, so we got quite the deal venturing into the mountains with only the expense of a backpack full of goodies. We hiked into the pine forests to find a perfectly secluded spot for a picnic. I'd lay out a blanket, we'd set up our humble hors d'oeuvres, pop open a bottle of wine ... and *converse*. Our phones were off. Our minds and hearts were on. We discussed the latest happenings in our family drama, and we would strategize how to handle our troubles. This was so, so important to dealing with our social smear. But more importantly, this gave us time to deal with how the social smear affected each of us — each of us differently — to help heal our relationship wherever we fell short.

We found our favorite spots. One was quite far in on a wooded peak that gave us a peering view between two other peaks, like pillars on each side of an overlook to the Monument valley. It would have been perfect if it wasn't for a lone, dead tree spearing up through our majestic view. So one day I brought a hatchet with us. I chopped it down as Wendy cheered me on. It was at least 10 inches thick, so it was no easy task. Wendy drank her wine while I huffed and puffed and sweated. She laughed at me as I swung, chop after chop. But when it fell, we cheered together, our cheers echoing into the wild. Now the view was wide open and free of death. I laid back on the blanket in exhaustion, proud of my triumph, so happy to have my wife believing in me again. We made love on the blanket, then sharing more wine with cheese and crackers. What a wonderful moment in our marriage.

Let me take a moment to speak to the couple "facing hate," whatever the social smear or family trauma. Do not let your marriage crumble. There will be temptations to abandon each other, the thought being that ruin with your partner is the lesser of two evils. Don't believe it. Resist with all of your heart and strength! Cleve to each other by finding your escape routes of joy. For Wendy and me, it was a cheap bottle of wine with some picnic munchies. We had God's beautiful Pikes National Forest to venture into. You have other spots. Other places. Wherever God leads you, go. Never let the wedge of separation tempt you into thinking a better path exists. You and your beloved will make it through this terrible time, and you will be stronger together.

I haven't yet shared much about my spiritual predicament through all of this. Honestly, I'm not proud of it. I had been a professing Christian since I was 17, quite the heralded spiritual leader in my circle of friends and, later, the Christian publishing world. You would think I would overcome my depressing circumstances — like so many patriarchs of scripture, martyrs of the faith, even Jesus Christ himself. I always anticipated myself responding to life's unfair persecution in similar fashion as them.

Instead, I had become such a pathetic let-down. I felt like God had become an uncaring deity intentionally putting me through immense pain, forcing me to my knees crying for mercy. I recall a screaming prayer that seemed nearly blasphemous at the time. "Enough!" I raged through clenched teeth, as if I should be commanding the Creator of the Universe. I was dangerously upset with my Lord and Savior. My religious friends would try to console me. "God will make you stronger through this trial," was a common, carefree attempt at encouragement. Thanks, but no thanks. Here was another spiritual cliché: "God doesn't give you a cross you can't carry." Are you kidding me?! If the life of public shame and humility was somehow the life God had ordained for me, I didn't want any of it. My faith shriveled and froze to the nihilistic depravity of an angry, agnostic unbeliever.

I now realize that this was precisely where God wanted me, but for a long while I thought it was a divine act of cruelty. I'm glad to say that just like my marriage did not crumble, neither did my faith in God. I cannot say it was easy, pleasant or even merely *hard*. And it was hardly pristine. You may reject my view of the divine if you like; we can still be friends and learn together from my exit from my social smear. But please don't reject my story simply because I profess faith in a God who cares more for me than I do for myself. My story has much to say about the tumultuous world of social smearing. I cannot, however, get away from the miraculous removal of the dark mountain that loomed before me.

Though I was locked away in my prison cell of shame, miracles — yes, out-of-this-world miracles — came about that I could not have possibly orchestrated myself. Just look at my story so far: it seems so unbelievable that it appears fabricated. Seriously, I just "ran into" my daughter at a Rush concert thronged by 20,000 fans? I had just been talking about a strategy of what to do when I might meet her? And my other daughters just "happen" to court men who counsel them back to my home? Were these "coincidences"? Just chance happenings?

Wendy and I spent many hikes talking of such things. Her faith was always stronger than mine, and she seemed to think I should let go of my circumstances and be just as strong. Forgive me, wife of my youth, but I found this difficult to do. I felt abandoned and betrayed. This was not the trial I signed up for! Drag me into the street and threaten my life. Fine. But strip my family from me and ravage my reputation online? I didn't foresee this trauma, and I want no part of it.

One of our ventures into the national forest was the day before Valentine's Day. Love wasn't on our minds, but we trudged loyally into the forest together. Our hearts were in a tender and vulnerable place. We had shared several deep cries at the top of the mountain peaks over the previous winter. If God was with us, he was with us in the mountains, in the wild, at those heartbreaking moments.

Being the day before Valentine's Day, we gave ourselves a bit more time. We ventured off the beaten trail and cleared a small peak on the backside of Mt. Herman. It seems like every rock has its own character, and the rocks we carried in our chests in place of our hearts were the most unique among them. Our mood was an awkward mix of glee and glumness, enjoying our hike but mourning our social smear. We didn't see much hope in our situation at the time.

We took an alternate way down. Great boulders peppered this side of the mountain as we zigzagged our way toward home. We climbed one small hump to dead-end into a giant rock three times the size of any man. It was such a surprise! We stood in near disbelief, not believing our eyes at first. The bolder was a near-perfect shape of a heart, standing straight above us, hidden from the main trail but clear as day before us now. "Look, Wendy!" I cried. "It's our Valentine's Day rock!" We laughed and then cried at this discovery we could have easily missed walking by in our sorrow.

I suppose there are a million metaphors we could have drawn from this discovery. Are we hardened? Are we hiding our true hearts? Is God showing us something wrong that we should take notice of? Here's what I think. God wanted to show us that he's got our hearts on his mind. It wasn't a harsh or hard or hindering sign. It was playful. Millennia ago, God dropped this heart-shaped rock in the middle of a million-acre forest, and he already knew that two middle-aged lovers would walk by it on the eve of Valentine's Day. It is a massive boulder to us, but to him it was a tiny dab from his creative brush. I envision him smiling when he tucked this boulder into the side of our mountain.

This was just like God as I once knew him. He has a sense of humor, showing himself in simple ways that urge me to ponder his greatness and his friendship. I may not have my life figured out, but God does. He's okay with my questions and my doubts, and he's got Wendy and me in the palm of his hands. He's the Ultimate Gamer, leading us to higher land in the tumultuous waters of life. I wasn't sure where this journey was going to take me, but God wasn't about to let me go. He seemed to want to let me know that he had my back, and that this difficulty was not going to go to waste. It was impossible for him to do otherwise. His love was settled, like a rock.

I know how devastating social smearing can be, but there is hope, and it is in the truth. "The truth will set you free," Jesus said two millennia ago, and his words ring true more so today than ever. I have found that when I center on the truth of a smear — no matter how outlandish or dramatically false — I have overcome the damage of the smear, learned more about myself and my relationships with others, and even reconciled with those who have participated in the initial attacks. I hope this resonates with all those suffering the impacts of social smearing — ruined reputations, divorces, lost careers, devastated lives — because I believe I have found the path out of the darkness you're experiencing.

I was beginning to see the light at the end of the tunnel. There was a purpose to my trial through social smearing. Or, perhaps, God was going to use this social smear to do something big. Now *that's* a walk I signed onto when I became a Christian years ago. To do something big, to show others the saving grace of Christ, to bring heaven on earth. That's what God had in mind for me, my family and even those couple of daughters who remained in the clench of darkness.

When you're presented with the unbelievable — that which is impossible and shakes your understanding of life and how the world works — you run the risk of embracing unbelief itself. This is what nearly ruined me, but God helped me overcome my doubts. I had children who were possessed with some sort of wicked interpretation of life, much like the demon-possessed mentioned in the bible. I'm not one to look for demons behind every bush or even to suggest that my daughters had succumbed to demonic influence, but I identify with the father in the book of Mark who begged Jesus to heal his son of his possession. Jesus' answer? *Belief.* "Everything is possible for one who believes," he said. I now, more than ever, understand this dad's response: "I do believe; help me overcome my unbelief!" (Mark 9:23-24).

Just in case you're struggling to believe this mountain-moving story, I took a picture of our beloved Heart Rock as proof. I also have a photo of my daughter and me at the Rush concert, along with wedding pix from my other daughter's magnificent mountain nuptials that included our whole family. Tucked away in digital folders and physical albums are also countless images of my smiling family living everyday life while showing the love and joy that is so much the truth of who we are. The truth does matter, and the truth is *we are not abusers.* We are a large, loving family. We look out for one another and protect one another. I'll yell it from the mountaintop: *Chris and Wendy Jeub are good parents who do their level best to help and love and guide their many beautiful blessings through the difficulties of life.* The proof is in the pictures. The truth is there for all to see.

The LORD is my rock, my fortress and my deliverer; my God is my rock, in whom I take refuge, my shield and the horn of my salvation, my stronghold.

—Psalm 18:2

Chapter 7: Hiring the Smeared

Early in our marriage, Wendy and I set a goal to travel from coast to coast with the children. But my first teaching job paid a depressing $14,900 per year. It would take a miracle to fulfill our far-ranging dream. Still, we were filled with love and optimism, so why not set the goalpost high and aim for it? Wendy and I prayed for this impossible goal to be met, and we were most confident it would be fulfilled. Our plan? We figured I'd write a bestseller and we'd use the funds to spend on a cross-country road trip. Perhaps God saw my first draft and wasn't impressed, so he came up with an alternative plan.

You may recall that I had a frustrating time settling into the teaching profession in the late '90s. I taught in three districts over five years, never fitting into the various dramas of the public school system. I loved teaching, but the political and administrative hassles made the career difficult to tolerate. I started a small business on the side, creating source material for academic debaters. Students — particularly homeschoolers — bought it up. So began an audience of homeschool debaters, and I became the sole publisher of source material for the small market.

I traveled to national tournaments during the summers of '99 and 2000, and wouldn't you know it? God blessed our goal. The first trip was to Virginia. My family vacationed in Washington, D.C., swam in the coastal waters of Virginia Beach and even got to attend the groundbreaking ceremony of Patrick Henry College. The next year we traveled to Point Loma, Calif., for the launch of the now-popular NCFCA homeschool speech and debate league. We camped at Yellowstone, visited Colorado Springs, and — of course! — swam in the warm water near San Diego. Coast to coast in a year. Prayers answered, in style.

I left the teaching profession in '00 after a district layoff, moved my family to Colorado, and served another professional stint as a Senior Online Editor at Focus on the Family. I learned much about the world of publishing, made several connections in its world and even picked up an MBA. I officially merged my three worlds — teacher, publisher and businessman — when I left full-time employment in 2004 to grow my own curriculum-development business. Monument Publishing was incorporated and remains in service today.

Several other opportunities opened up along the years of this journey, even buying a school bus and converting it into an RV — called a "schoolie" to bus-conversion fans — to keep us traveling the country. Our family ran debate camps in Idaho, Oregon, California, Texas, Florida, Virginia, the Carolinas and, of course, our own state of Colorado. Our kids became the most cultured American kids ever, seeing most of the country and growing their communication skills along the way. Self-employment and homeschooling allowed us tremendous flexibility to gather the kids and head off to whatever tournament I could plug them into — and I typically would bring my books in tow to sell along the way. My "traveling show" was speech-and-debate source material for other homeschool families. As speech and debate grew in popularity, my revenue grew. I applied my editing skills to assemble the best materials for these families to grow their own programs.

I had big plans in the works pre-2014: a major business acquisition, a unique camp tailored to debate graduates, and public speaking tours. They all fell through as a result of my public shaming. As I asked earlier, would you send your kid to a debate camp led by someone accused of abuse? I wouldn't either, no matter how innocent he might actually be. Our training camps were a major part of my revenue-building plan, and it came to a slothful slow after 2014, never reaching capacity again. Publishing still clunked along, but nothing compared to the roaring years prior to the smear.

An enjoyable aspect of self-employment is my ability to be generous with my time and resources. For years I volunteered at our local homeschool co-op — an assembly of approximately 350 students and their parents — teaching that which I loved and knew best: writing. I was perhaps the most overqualified teacher there, most others being homeschool moms, who, while being creative and intelligent, were not certified, degree-carrying professional teachers. When my social smear hit, I came under the scrutiny of the board and even had some of them sit in to monitor my small classes. I don't blame them, really. These members knew me and they knew the truth, but they needed to consider the liability I now was. How embarrassing and unfair! Coupled with the fact that I made no money teaching there, I soon found that I could not continue.

I cannot express how difficult it is to let go of 14 years of self-employment, but my bread-winning ability was at its end. Finances were tightening, and Wendy and I needed to find a way to make more money. Though some of our children were adults, living their lives successfully away from us, we still had many more kids at home. Some were in a local charter school, some attended an early-college program, and some were being schooled at home. It was a complicated schedule for a large family, one that Wendy and I had dedicated to God years before, and we were back to hoping for a miracle to make it all work out.

You may have noticed that I have withheld the names of my children from my story. I spent long hours agonizing over whether to use their names or not. Frankly, the tale would have been much easier to tell had I used them. And certainly if I were writing a book of fiction, names would have been at the forefront. But I have no wish to single any of my children out for blame, repercussions or shame. I love each of them dearly, and though their allegations against me are false, I do not want to publicly rebuke them, even by way of a simple rebuttal. Frankly, I am more interested in the day of reconciliation in our personal family matter, and I wholeheartedly believe that day will come. In time.

Reconciliation or not, my focus eventually turned to survival. No matter where a person is on the spectrum of income, social smearing can devastate you. Even the rich and famous — typically accustomed to public shaming, or so we think — feel the financial impact of fabrications against them. Whether you're rich or poor, you have made a living for yourself, but the money likely stops when you are shamed, certainly so if you are accused of crimes. I didn't have a "regular" job to keep me afloat, and my residual income dwindled as the social smearing campaign carried on. I catered to a specific audience, and when that audience held back their support for the work I did, I had to readjust my lifestyle and my business. Those who suffer social smearing often have no other choice.

Another inherent problem with being socially smeared: You never really know who knows what. Some people (wisely) shut off social media altogether. Others — many others — don't, and they search to know every juicy detail of your personal life, all colored by the perspective of your smearer. This reality made it difficult for me to seek supplemental work. I had several assets at my disposal — an MBA with an emphasis on electronic communications, an English bachelor's degree merely an online application away from a teaching certificate, over a decade of small business development and management — but who's to say a Google search wouldn't ruin my opportunities? *Jeub* is a very rare name, and for several years disparaging blog posts came up on Page 1. Search "Chris Jeub" and tabloid articles "exposing the truth" of my abusive tendencies rose to the top. My squeaky-clean legal record meant nothing, and my strong résumé fell far short when looked at side by side with the online fabrications. This was the new normal for my life.

I pressed on the best I could, pursuing three avenues simultaneously. The first was what I had always done if I felt tight with finances: gin up a new product or service of some sort. This is the flexibility and ability of most experienced and resourceful entrepreneurs — unless you've been socially smeared. I launched a few ideas, but they met the same resistance as my current business, so nothing took off. The second was something in line with internet development, with which I had extensive experience and knowledge. I targeted some companies in Colorado Springs that had plenty of openings and great opportunities, but I never received a response for any of the positions. I felt ignored, and I couldn't help but think that these internet companies were at least savvy enough to do a quick Google search on its candidates. Who would hire an accused abuser? Not internet companies, apparently. I eventually turned to my third avenue: teaching.

Luckily for me, teaching was an increasing need in Colorado. I had let my certificate expire years ago, but the Colorado Department of Education was under pressure to quickly recertify people like me. My curriculum publishing easily served to update my continuing education requirements. So I renewed my teaching certificate and began applying for jobs. In the meantime, I taught as a substitute in several area districts.

I was fingerprinted by the local police as part of the process teachers in Colorado undergo. All districts do a standard background check on every applicant, a requirement by law for all public, charter and private schools. Even the homeschool co-op I previously volunteered for did a background check. I was never convicted or even accused of a crime, as you know. My record was as clean as a whistle. This cleared the runway for me to teach again, and every school is desperate for substitutes. But human resource departments give more scrutiny before hiring a full-time teacher. Again, the thought haunted me: Whomever did the hiring for a given school I applied to would search my name online and then remove me from their small list of applicants without ever explaining why.

I had one thing going for me: my relationship with our local charter school. My children attended, six of nearly 1,000 students in the K-8 school. We were the largest family in the school, and though we were Christian homeschool leaders, we were welcomed in the charter school culture. My children did well in this environment, and the teachers got to know me through my kids, as most teachers do. One of my sons, in fact, won the highest honor of the 1st-grade class: the school's motto award, which is given to the student voted most exemplary of the behaviors promoted by the "Character First" school. We felt the academy was welcoming of us and, if they happened to know of it, sympathized with us over our online trial.

I had assumed the administration knew of my social smear, as the vice principal got the early story back when my daughter visited the campus uninvited. He, however, had moved positions to the elementary grades. I was interested in the middle school. Teachers started to get to know me as I enthusiastically embraced substitute teaching, on call every morning to pick up whatever lesson the teacher left for me. I subbed for other schools, but my favorite was the one my kids attended. I loved its Core Knowledge sequence, its Character First program, its conservative take on literature and history, and its professional atmosphere. Besides, since my younger children attended, carpooling back and forth from home was extremely convenient.

Remember my encouragement earlier to "walk in the truth"? I could not allow my social smear to prevent me from that which I deserved ... and I deserved to fairly and truthfully pursue a teaching job. The socially smeared are greatly tempted to submit to the accusations and fabrications, hold their head in shame while anticipating that — though undeserved or untrue — others will not approve of their reputations. Teachers are governors of children, and though I was never formally accused of a crime and certainly never convicted, the reputations of teachers precede them. If the school followed social media at all, I certainly would not be a candidate for teaching there.

It turns out that the charter school discouraged social media among its administration and teaching staff, as I believe every school should. (You will see why later.) This opened the doors for me to be hired. A long-term substitute position opened up at the end of the school year, and the dean asked me to finish the year off for them. This placed me as a top candidate for the following year. My license was renewed, my credentials were in order, and I finished out the school year teaching an English class. I loved it! I was even able to "strut my stuff" a bit, teaching writing to the kids, getting to connect with some key parents in the school, and earning the respect of the administration and other middle school teachers. Getting hired for the following year was a cakewalk, I figured.

I was wrong, however, to assume that my new administration knew my full story, or to assume they would be on my side. I had made grandiose plans to spend my summer organizing my business affairs in order to begin my first year of English teaching since I left the profession 18 years before. But these plans were brought to an abrupt stop when, in early June, a parent caught wind of my online accusations and — rather than bringing her concerns to the administration — reposted onto the school's Facebook pages every juicy bit of gossip she could find on Google. Hundreds of families attend the charter school, most of whom did not know us personally, and they were being told that the school "hired an abuser." I was four years separated from the social blowup of 2014, hoping that it could finally be relegated to the past, but that's not how social smears work. They say the internet is forever, and it seemed my trial would never end. One parent was all it took to whip up the social smear all over again. She started her own Facebook group she called "Concerned Parents" of the school, and she was determined to find me guilty as charged. I was about to walk through this valley of persecution and misery all over again.

I had a lot more going for me in 2018 than I did in 2014. This administration knew me, the teachers knew my children, and I had proven myself in the classroom. We had several close friends involved in the charter school, which, by the way, is a "charter of parents." Parents served on the school board and were more involved than your standard public school parent. Some already knew of and sympathized with our predicament with our oldest daughters.

I was called into the office at school for a meeting. I was the fifth person in the room, gathered together with four administrators. They informed me that they'd read what was posted online but wanted my side of the story before taking any formal action. I can only imagine that they were considering firing me, even before I'd really started. I explained everything as best I could, starting all the way back to the 2014 social smear, how this trauma had devastated my family, how we had worked hard for nearly four years to overcome the trial. I doggedly tried my best not to point fingers and keep my presentation as sincere as possible. I pegged the ordeal as a "personal family matter" that was "four years old," a story of "estranged daughters" who took to social media to smear their parents. By this time only one daughter still remained true to the fabricated online narrative — even the oldest who was still estranged no longer supported her sister — which made things fairly conclusive, 15 voices to one.

Outside our meeting I had several people coming to my defense. One in particular was a student from the previous year. "I learned more about writing than I ever had," she testified. An active parent of the school, one who had been a close friend of Wendy's for many years, wrote a letter to the administration and school board, affirming the falsity of the online accusations against me. A former school board member had a son who befriended my son and whose family had had us over to their home more than once; this dad became a phone-calling lobbyist for my defense. Perhaps most helpful was a personal letter from my formerly "predatory" daughter, the one you met in Chapter 5. Now, as you know, she was married and had a son of her own. Here is her appeal to the administration and school board:

> *To whom it may concern,*
>
> *I am Chris and Wendy Jeub's 4th child and was a supporter of my sister's public blog post outburst 4 years ago that changed a lot of things for all of us Jeubs.*
>
> *I would like to present a separate perspective to the story that is out for the public to read. At the time I wholeheartedly supported my sister's story but now with a few years of adulting behind me and a voice of my own that I've never let freely speak about it, there's some serious things worth looking at when those who are directly impacted (my dad, my mom and my siblings) are battling these rumors and upsets with people in their personal lives.*
>
> *First off, my dad's record is 'squeaky clean,' my family has never had an issue from CPS or the police in any way regarding the care and safety of their children. Some phone calls have been made by people who don't know my family personally, but no charges and no evidence. Ever.*

Secondly... I want to address Media, Publicity, Rumors and Gossip in their relation to the personal lives of a very unique and uncommon family dynamic, such as mine. No one knows my family like those who have lived and live there and those close friends we have had over the years.

Thirdly, I want to write about my 4 years of adult life away from home. I had no idea what "abuse" was or the true ugliness and injustice of what it could look like. I most certainly didn't understand what it is to survive on my own or to take care of and support a little-one in more ways than changing some diapers and other things I learned growing up with so many little siblings. The story of my childhood is filled with much joy, freedom to be a kid and plenty of love and support in the ways my parents knew how to give it. After learning some different childhood realities I was smacked in the face with the truth of mine: I was free to be me. I was supported financially. I always had a roof over my head and food in my belly (which I didn't appreciate fully until I had to work for those basics myself). My parents gave me a foundation of good morals I still stick to today. I and my little siblings agree we had room to dream and knew we could believe in ourselves to be great and do great things. What I've learned is: very few families get that. Very few ADULTS had that kind of a steady upbringing. My Mom did it all with 15 pregnancies and 16 children to care for. My dad took this responsibility HEAD ON, adopted my two oldest sisters and became a present and providing father for all of us as our family developed. I've been a parent 2 short years and I can't count the mistakes I've made. Boy am I grateful for the wisdom and little tidbits of advice my parents have from their experience as parents: Their mistakes, mishaps, personal things that come up and so much more that have shaped the life they have today. That is, in my opinion, evolving to beautiful new experiences for my siblings at home and to me who gets to visit and sleep and eat there whenever.

For those who haven't experienced a family of as many closely-aged siblings as my family's household, I have to share some of the beauty I see for our future. My family's environment at home, I believe, is only going to get more fun, more eventful and more loving as we grow and improve and challenge each other as adults and all have our own kids. I often imagine what it will be like in 15 years or even just 3-5 years with marriages, babies being born and individual careers developing for all the Jeub Teens, Jeub adults/parents, Jeub Grandkids and Jeub in-laws. Also the close friends who have stuck by my parents through thick and thin.

This backlash in my parents' personal lives (affecting new friends, my dad's job, distrust from strangers, odd questions from people at my little siblings school they shouldn't have to be asked OR try to answer) is something that comes along with being in the spotlight, even if the cameras have been gone for years. There's going to be people who don't believe in us, who judge, who question, who gossip, who say all sorts of unwarranted hurtful things. If your privacy were the rug under your feet, life in the spotlight just tore it out from under you and broke some bones.

As my relationship with my parents smoothed, I've learned it's important not to suppress issues in the family but it's also very important to have a place for healing that's NOT public. A trusting zone to heal, open up, appreciate, be accepting, understanding and supportive of the other family members and who they are.

The Jeub home is a wonderful place to be. Everyone's always doing something, someone's always home, somebody's always making food. It's a place I can go anytime. A place I will be fed, gifted, clothed (my mom and my three teenage sisters all have clothes that fit! Woohoo!), loved, conversed with, hugged, made to laugh, inspired, asked if I'm okay, asked a million questions (I have to filter which ones to put energy into answering and which ones to just not or I'm way too burnt out, lol) and just so so SO much more. It's wonderful to have a relationship with my mom and to have her support and advice. My mom is a social butterfly and her friends would agree; a great friend to have! She's fun and reliable, scheduled and dependable, happy and giving, resourceful and loving.

My dad is one who cooks, cleans, serves and teaches. He's incredibly Loyal and the responsibilities he takes on in life are from the heart. He's organized, intelligent, welcoming and giving.

It's incredible to watch the sons he raised turn into such responsible adults with problem solving skills and a healthy drive to pursue their dreams with passion and class.

My heart could burst when I watch the effect this place has had on my toddler. He turns into the happiest, most energetic, excited, VIBRANT little boy ever and always sleeps and eats well.

I could go on and on. The fact is, my family is truly amazing and I'm so grateful to have them.

Wow! Finally, words from my daughter that expressed the real love in my family. This letter was a cool, fresh cleansing that brought me to tears. And on a practical level, it's not a bad defense, wouldn't you say? Like I said,

I had so much more going for me than I did in 2014 when the smear first hit the internet. Today the drama seemed like old news, a past personal trial that, if anything, strangers might even sympathize with me instead of holding me in contempt.

At least this is what those of us who are socially smeared hope for. But in a world where "truth doesn't matter" and you have one (or perhaps a few) social warriors with their cell phones ready to serve up more mounds of mob "justice," you are never fully absolved. I had a strong defense — friends testifying, school leaders lobbying, former students validating, and even one of my former smearers recanting her story and elaborating on what a great dad I was — but it still amounted to very little in the world of social smearing. No defense was good enough to convince the mob to back off.

The parent who initially raised the concern worked diligently to rally other parents to her side. She attempted to make her group look bigger than it was, but it became obvious that she was drawing in outside sources — people unaffiliated with the school or even our town — and making empty claims that "hundreds" of concerned parents were siding with her. She never once attempted to reach out to the principal, and certainly not to me. She relied entirely on the gossip she gathered and redistributed on the internet, primarily through her new Facebook group. The number of members amounted to no more than 42, and more than half of them dropped off without ever engaging in the forum. In the end, I estimated that only three moms were the agitators.

Litigation was considered. These moms weren't my children, so I had no problem suing them for libel and public defamation, and likely winning. But these moms were moms of kids in the school where I wanted to teach, and litigation would draw in the press and likely make a public scene the school definitely did not want. As things stood at the time, we were like a family squabbling amongst ourselves, and avoiding litigation was clearly best for the school. Just like litigation would have torn my family apart four years prior, lawsuits had the potential to tear our charter school apart. At the very *best*, it would make my first year of teaching dead on arrival.

Of course I did not hold these moms in high esteem, but I had come a long way in my personal understanding of social smearers. I may have seen them as personal enemies, taking the word of gossips over the word of a respected teacher. However, they see themselves as whistleblowers, advocates for a better community, "Concerned Parents" of the school their children attend. I had learned how to love my enemies, and perhaps there was a way to untie this newly formed "bond of three not easily broken." As you know, I had dealt with this impossibility before, and if there was a way to turn one or perhaps two away from their online hatred, this could all be worked out for the good of the school.

One of the "bond of three" mothers happened to be the next-door neighbor of one of my closest advocates. My friend took the initiative to assemble a meeting of three couples at their home: Wendy and me, my friend and his wife, and the husband and "concerned" social-smearing wife. I was going to be the English teacher of their children, and my friend couched the meeting wisely. "We have concerns over Mr. Jeub," he started. "I know Chris and Wendy to a certain degree, but I am worried over what kind of teacher the school hired, so I assembled the meeting to openly discuss things." He was more an advocate for me than he let on, but for the sake of persuading the social-smearing parents — particularly the mother — my friend positioned himself as having like-minded concerns.

The meeting was a fantastic three hours of expressing concerns and overcoming doubts. I explained my family's story much like I had done with my administrators. Wendy was able to add a motherly touch and speak affection into our dilemma. And it turned out that this mother was not concerned so much with the accusation of abuse, but more so that I was a "reality TV star" who held to conservative Christian beliefs. I took time to explain my views, as they were not as "alt-right" as she had been led to believe. This was the first time she got to meet me, her opinion being formed solely by the garbage written about me online. In our meeting we discussed two articles that this mother had her biggest problems with, articles that made it sound like I was a patriarch who didn't believe girls should be educated. What nonsense! It didn't take much to reason through the articles from years ago, how context brought meaning to their topics, and it was clearly understood by the end of our get-together that while I may have been a "reality TV star," I certainly was not the patriarchal cheuvenist she had thought. We left our meeting overturning every stone of concern this mother had. She even hugged Wendy before she left, saying, "I made a new friend tonight."

This mother returned to Facebook and took down all her hurtful accusations against me, which was good. But I had hoped she would turn out to be a vocal online advocate. This is a reality of the socially smeared. Even when you've been vindicated, and even when your adversaries turn to your favor, it is very, very rare for any public apology or retraction to be offered. Wendy's "new friend" removed her bombastic Facebook posts but still asked for my removal. "The school should not hire someone so controversial," was her new stand. It was better than being nailed to the wall for fabricated lies about being an abusive dad, but it was not a complete turn, and it was not a total win.

My "win" came June 21, the night of a highly anticipated board meeting. Wendy and I had been traveling from Minneapolis to Dallas on a small business trip we had planned, part of our reordering of our business affairs to prepare for my year of teaching. We knew the board meeting would request the presence of the "bond of three," but the only one who could attend was Wendy's "new friend," once viciously hostile but now much more docile about her views. She reiterated for the public record the same new position she had taken on the Facebook page, that she had reservations for my hire, but her objection did not go very far. She was followed by the satisfied parent of the student who appealed earlier, and her impact was powerfully positive. "Mr. Jeub is controversial to some," she is on record as saying, "but Dr. Martin Luther King Jr. was considered controversial, too. Controversy should not be a criteria when hiring."

The board unanimously decided to keep me on. I didn't hear the news till we were driving through Illinois. We received an email from the board president, sent to the entire parent list of the charter and later published in our town newspaper, here in partiality:

After a careful review of various social media postings and direct expressions of concern by families, along with the facts and documentation presented by school leadership and reviewed by the school's legal counsel, the Board agrees with Administration that the issues raised in connection with a recent employment matter fall within three categories:

1) issues not relevant to employment at [the school], including personal matters protected under both federal and state antidiscrimination laws;

2) issues that clearly support the hiring decision and reflect the fact that the hiring decision was not only justifiable, but was exceedingly so; or

3) issues that upon further investigation were found to be false and malicious.

It was so refreshing to read someone finally calling my smear "false and malicious." We won this fight, and we won it big; the first confident win in four years of social smearing. Wendy and I pulled over on the highway and cried. It was such a tremendous victory to be kept on by the school, and remarkably vindicating for the board to recognize the allegations as "false and malicious."

I went back to my plan: wrap up my business affairs and enter full-time teaching in August. It was a relatively quiet two months of work, and I was yet again naively hopeful that my social smear would not return. But of course it did. These parents did not go silent into the night. They may have lost the fight on their Facebook page, and they may have lost the fight with the school board, but they were not done with me. They were now taking their fight to one more battle ground, the major newspaper in Colorado Springs, *The Gazette*.

Teachers returned to school in early August for two weeks of training and preparation before the students arrived. On August 15, still in training with the open house soon to come, I made the front page of the paper: "Monument parents upset with hiring former reality TV star as a teacher." It became one of the hottest articles of the summer, generating over 400 heated comments and thousands of online shares. Local radio picked up the story and made it a major talking point of the week. Three parents were quoted in the article — the "bond of three" — and all three threatened to protest my classroom during our open house and then sit in my classroom during class hours ... to make sure Chris Jeub didn't "abuse" their kids.

The embarrassment of my social smear had now officially become a tumultuous trial for the school that had hired me. My plan for a smooth return to teaching was about to change.

Gossip on social media is one thing. When "real" media like the town's newspaper picks it up, your job is on the line.

Chapter 8: The Right to Overcome

I would not have blamed any administration to drop me like a hot potato. I was a social media storm brewing among the parents of my charter school, and there was little to win in keeping me on as a teacher. School administrations are no different than most organizations, and boards act in accordance with what is best for the school. When someone proves to be an embarrassment to the greater organization, the managers work with HR to figure out a way to get rid of the problem. It doesn't always matter what the truth is, nor what the bosses personally believe. Who hasn't seen these situations work this way? Fair or unfair, for better or worse, political issues like me get moved out, we are "cancelled," for the greater good, one supposes.

Charter schools are different, though, and my administrators were incredible professionals. More than once the directors affirmed their commitment to the truth, to doing the right thing, to stand by one of their teachers who was getting unfairly slammed online. I'm sure they had their moments of doubt, but they had a fighting spirit about them that made them charter school advocates in the first place. As I've already shared, I was a homeschool advocate who bucked the system over the years, and these charter school leaders were also accustomed to fighting the system. Like homeschoolers, they raged against the machine of the behemoth public education system. They were freedom-seeking educators who fought hard to take back what the state didn't deserve: the right of parents to educate their own children. I loved (and still love) being a part of their family of parents and educators.

That is the atmosphere of the charter school. But not all participating parents are always of the same mind. In this case, three in particular were hell-bent on forcing the school's hand to remove me from teaching. These were the same three who smeared my name all over again on the Facebook walls of the school, attempting diligently to rally a mob against my hiring. The truth didn't seem to matter to these parents, and they used social smearing as their weapon to tear up the town. They didn't just come after me, they came after anyone who attempted to seek the truth of the matter, very much like the bad ol' days of 2014 when the initial smear ravaged my life. Anyone appearing to support me or the administration was harassed even more.

One of the three reposted a tabloid article written about my family in 2014, along with this comment: "Mr. Jeub reportedly has been hired to teach English in the fall. Where is the common sense and judgment??? This man WILL NOT teach my daughter and I seriously question the character of those who would believe this man belongs in the classroom teaching children. Please speak out, email, scream from the rooftops NO!"

This post was out there for all the school's parents to read. I had learned much over the previous four years, knowing well enough *not* to engage. The truth did not matter, remember, so any explanation would fall short. Another mom, someone we did not know, challenged the comment: "This is not the way to air this out, you should go directly to the school and express your concerns. You should get the facts first before ruining [the teacher's] chances. This article was written in 2014, and it's a gossip magazine."

Within minutes, another mom — one of the three who led this smearing campaign — continued the thread: "This man has already been hired by the school. He is on record as being a Fundamental Christian...if you aren't aware of the facts surrounding what they teach...please research." Another of the three added, "There is an underlying intolerance towards kids who don't have faith. I've seen it and my kids who actually do have faith, but not the right kind, have experienced it in the form of comments, and attitude. It's very insidious."

Do you see how wound up this was becoming? Social smearing works that way. These parents surely saw themselves as whistleblowers, exposing that which the powers-at-hand were "covering up." But the administration and board weren't covering anything up! Every little detail of my life had been exposed for the world to see. But social smearers do not hold the truth as a counterweight. Any attempt to speak reason into the social media windstorm quickly turns on you. If you try — and I am grateful many people did try — you became the defendant somehow justifying the installment of a "convicted abuser" in a school classroom.

As you know, the school didn't budge. This was the biggest victory of my four years of being socially smeared. I finally had a governing body rationally analyzing the data, formulating a truthful verdict, and then sticking with the right side of the issue. They were fully convinced that I was unjustly accused, even calling out my smears as "false and malicious," and they held firm with their decision. I was going to be an English teacher for the school, and I deserved it!

And then yet another shoe dropped: front-page coverage in the Colorado Springs *Gazette. How many feet did this monster have?*

Our academy had inservice meetings for two weeks leading up to the first day of school, which included an open house for parents to come meet the teachers. I had become the gossip of the school, no doubt interesting gab-fodder for many. I wanted none of it. Neither did my bosses, and they did all they could to make sure I was protected from the social mob infiltrating the school. The three "concerned parents" posted messages about how they wanted to sit in my classroom when school started, or perhaps have their children be excused entirely from my English class, but none of these requests ever materialized. Our charter school was a "school of choice," so these parents always had a way out by pulling their kids and going elsewhere. They didn't. And neither did any other parent of the nearly 1,000 enrolled students.

This should settle nicely for those of you who are socially smeared. The dragons are made of paper, roaring a scary roar but not nearly as impactful as you think. The social media hate that gets posted about you is, at first, shocking to your core. You tend to think everyone is in agreement with the mob. But even the leaders of the mob are weak, not nearly as strong as they appear online. The proof for me was how many outraged parents actually yanked their kids from the charter school. Would you send *your* kid to a classroom commanded by a felony-level abuser? Turns out not one parent of my 120 middle school students thought such things were actually true, taking action by removing their own kids from the danger such a situation would indicate. Not even the "bond of three" moms withdrew their children.

Another word of truth from someone who has been dragged through social smearing hell: Your adversaries are probably not upset with what they say they are upset with. Remember when I was talking about how I had to learn the fine art of "leaning in"? There were underlying problems with my family that had nothing to do with abuse or neglect. If I had only focused on these false accusations, I likely would have lost all hope, especially when it came to reconciling with my daughters. The same was true with the three parents upset about my teaching their kids. They used the accusation of abuse against me, but that wasn't their real beef with me, and I don't even think they believed it. They were upset with me for other things, as you will soon see, and smearing me was their way to seek "justice" for it.

I was still trying to wrap my head around these truths when one of the administrators stopped me in the hallway after work. "*The Gazette* called me asking about some parents," he said. "There may be an article coming." My heart sank. The director shared with me what he told the reporter — pretty much the same things we had dealt with earlier that summer — and said that the reporter may be contacting me for a follow-up.

She did, via email:

> Hi. I write for The Gazette, the daily newspaper in Colorado Springs. I'm doing a story about some parents upset about your hiring. Do you want to give a few comments? They primarily seem concerned about these two aspects: That your Christian faith might creep into your teaching, and that your previous blog posts on views about girls not needing to be as educated as boys will influence how you treat girls. As you know, they've said you are too controversial a figure to have at their school. Do you want to respond? I'm turning the story in later today.

Notice what is missing: *abuse*. You would think this would be the number-one issue with my teaching, but the reporter was instead getting an earful from "concerned parents" who didn't think this issue was as important as my Christian faith. And these parents never did seek a deeper understanding of me or my writings, as they would have then learned that I was an advocate for equal education no matter what the gender. These straw-man arguments were easy to deflate. The reporter left her phone number, but I did not call her. These pointed questions allowed me to zero in on brief, concise answers that, I hoped, the reporter would appreciate.

> Thank you for inquiring. Here are my answers to your questions.
>
> *That your Christian faith might creep into your teaching:*
>
> I have worked alongside countless Christians in my years of teaching, including here at the school. We are a charter school, not a Christian school, and I am fully aware how to teach in this environment.
>
> *... and that your previous blog posts on views about girls not needing to be as educated as boys will influence how you treat girls.*
>
> I have never advocated for an unequal education of boys and girls. Several years ago I blogged against a pastor who believed such nonsense. I have been quoted out of context for advocating for that which I have publicly stood against.

I spent time wordsmithing this response. I was purposefully succinct. If I were long-winded, the reporter could have selected parts of my response to reprint, and I didn't want that to happen. I was being strategic here, just as I had been with my daughters years earlier. My purpose was not to plead my case in its entirety, rehash every detail of my online smearing drama. It was to counter the media onslaught that was likely coming my way. The debate coach in me was on high alert.

She followed up with a question about the alleged abuse, as if it were merely a loose end:

> Last thing: What's your response to your daughter's allegations of abuse?

If I had been on high alert before, I was on DEFCON 4 now. In my estimation, this was the crux of the matter about my position at the charter school. If I was a Christian who was taken out of context for an article I wrote years ago, the school — especially this charter school — would wholeheartedly defend me. But if the courtroom of public opinion believed me to be an abuser, the school could buckle under the pressure. Where this would lead was anyone's guess. Facebook group whistleblowing was one thing, but now *real* media had picked up the story and was about to sound the alarm. Perhaps then parents would actually take the step of pulling their kids from the school. My response needed to put an end to the nonsense of my social smear, making it clear that I am as far from an abuser as the best of parents. Thankfully, this was not spin. This was the truth.

> The allegations were made four years ago and have proven to be false. I haven't made public rebuttals because, frankly, I am more interested in reconciliation with my daughter. This is a personal family matter that has been difficult on all of us.

The reporter ended up quoting me word for word, which is exactly what I hoped she would do. I cannot say for sure, but I imagine my three-mom adversary did not practice such brevity. Their major problem was with my Christian faith, and that did not hold water. Lots of teachers are Christians. So what? When the article dropped, all of us braced for the worst, but it ended up making the school administrators look like the freedom fighters that they were. For once I looked like the victim, targeted by a small group of disgruntled, Christian-hating parents who were harassing a popular and highly qualified English teacher.

A colleague of mine came over to congratulate me: "You are totally, 100% vindicated of all this smear." The administrator who connected me with the newspaper shared with me his opinion: "They gave it their best shot; they lost, we won, now let's get to work." The school was contacted by strangers encouraging them to "stick by the Christian teacher." A local radio show host spent all morning talking about "that English teacher" who was "getting beat up for his Christian faith," and phone call after phone call came in from supporters who found it appalling that a teacher was so cruelly attacked in the media. "These parents should be ashamed of themselves," one caller said. "He's one of their kids' teachers, and they're all bent out of shape about his Christian views."

And once again, notice what was missing: *abuse*. In the social smearing world, this had become an afterthought. The felony I committed was believing in Christ, not attacking my own children. Contrary to what nihilistic factions want to turn our country into, we are still a United States of America that values freedom of religion. And so it seemed that the accusation of "abuse" was indeed a straw man, easily knocked down. Once the true nature of the grievance was revealed, no one jumped onboard the "fire Jeub" bandwagon. And, again, no one took their kids out of school.

Do you think the smearers stopped their hate? You've come this far in my story, so you know the answer: Of course they didn't. During the open house, my administrators had to resort to guarding my door like security at a punk-band concert. As professionals they counted themselves as representatives of all the parents of the school, not just the few who tried to rally people to join them in their harassment. And that meant holding the worst offenders at bay. The social media posts continued, at least at the beginning of the year. Yet I quickly became a negative-news footnote.

I was a first-year teacher who should have focused his undivided attention on lesson work. I had curricula to consider, classroom procedures to set up, parents to email and call, and so much more. I had over 100 students who needed my attentiveness. Don't get me wrong, I love teaching and want nothing more than the best for all my students, but I had a social media storm rumbling over me, bumping and bruising me every time I considered my next teaching move.

So I taught straight as an arrow, seldom veering off the curricular path of the charter school. We had a clear sequence to follow, and any mention of God or even faith in general was delicately handled to avoid any accusation of "sharing my faith." In all honesty, I taught closely to how I would have taught without the smear in my life; I do not aspire to wholesale evangelism, and I would never proselytize students in the classroom. But even so, I was on pins and needles all year making sure the appearance wasn't even close. I had many meetings with my administrators on how to handle spiritual undertones in the curriculum's poetry and literature units, and whether to pursue deeper human themes that involve spirituality. These would have been healthy discussions in class, largely secular in nature but genuinely enlightening, but I was counseled to steer clear.

This is collateral damage to communities that suffer from social smearing. Most families at my school would have gladly welcomed deeper discussions in class, but our school was under attack from social warriors who would pounce on any approach that seemed to lean "right." The school also did not proceed with the debate program I had planned to lead. The administrators and I were fully focused on getting through the year. I would have loved to show my students the 2007 TLC show about my family, and I could have easily woven it into a healthy writing lesson. No way! I walked well within the boundaries, taught straight from the book, and ultimately my students had an "OK" teacher for the year. I could have been a far better, more enjoyable teacher had I the liberty to be so.

Instead, I had these few parents at my door demanding my removal. There were times my administration, I'm sure, felt more pressure than they admitted. A doubting voice inside my head often asked, "Are they ready to cave yet?" The gossip swirled online at precisely the same pace as my mind whirled. "Are they preparing to let me go?" was my fear. I recall one moment where I sent an email to my administrators expressing my appreciation for their support, and it was met with not a single reply. The silence was deafening, and the voice inside kept suggesting that ultimate defeat was around the corner.

Thankfully, my administration had my back, and my fears were one by one quenched by their sturdy support. They never let me down or wavered, repeatedly supporting me and resisting the pressure that came their way. This is rare in the world of social smearing, unfortunately. The powers-that-be often waver and weaken, obsessed with the associated damage that comes — no matter how unfair or untrue — on the heels of someone's tarnished reputation. Adults sometimes act like schoolchildren, alienating the one who is bullied or teased from fear of what others may think of them. Cliques exist among adults, too, and those of us smeared online often find ourselves sitting alone, unsupported, and outcast.

There were staff and prominent parents who — though they were not the social smearing agitators — did not welcome the negative press that had come with my hiring. One such person was a mother on the Parent Teacher Organization, whose views were exposed in a gossipy situation that involved a close friend of Wendy's. It created quite a stir, with some suspecting that there was some sort of "mole" among us. It led to an unfortunate breaking of a friendship that Wendy once held dear. Other, isolated flareups were handled professionally behind closed doors, but they were always emotionally draining and drew all of us away from our work. There was, for a few, a certain level of distrust in me and even the administration who supported me, and I couldn't help but feel like these were collegial betrayals.

But I had a unique advantage: One of my sons was one of my students. He was, in fact, close friends with the daughters of the "bond of three." I had feared that the children of my online smearing parents would videotape me or trick me into publicly indulging my faith or pester me into making some other error in judgment. Instead, they carried on as if nothing had happened, with no "gotcha" campaign ever surfacing. This was a pleasant surprise to my son and me, one that helped both of us get through a successful year — despite the online gossip that rolled on among the parents.

Ultimately, there were many players in this game that got us through the school-wide social smear — the administrators' professional insistence, the school board's denial of maliciousness, supportive parents far outnumbering the few who sought my demise. But I must credit these students for getting me through the school year. They were mature beyond their age, some refusing to follow in their parents' maligning footsteps. The social whirlwinds of emotionally wired middle schoolers have scant rhyme or reason, and maturity — especially the cognitive ability to reject conventional opinion, even from their own parents — is a rare commodity. My students could have so easily turned into savage little beasts determined to undermine my classroom, but they instead became some of my favorite *people*, not merely *pupils*.

An argument can be made that the school had a legal obligation to keep me on for at least the year they originally hired me for. They had no obligation to renew my contract, however. So when this administration, which diligently sought the truth, stood by its teachers and professionally strove to make the best school they could possibly make, offered me a second year's contract, I gladly and gratefully renewed. There was one more exciting thing that happened at the end of that first year at the charter school: my son, the one I mentioned was in my English class, was nominated for the grade's motto award. I recused myself from the voting, of course. And it was a major button-popping moment when he won! The other teachers later shared that his friendship with the children of the "bond of three" moms influenced them to grant him the award. He could have been a vigilante, looking to get revenge for how other families' parents treated his dad, but he chose the higher road of kindness and friendship. I'm so very proud of him, and proud of my colleagues who not only saw the truth but also embraced it.

All seemed to be ending well. I began entertaining the idea that perhaps my social smear was, in fact, going away. Not so fast, Jeub! Remember, in today's social media world, smears *never* go away. Hoping for such blissful release is a false hope; eventually, the dragon reappears and shakes its papier-mâché again. Sure enough, in March of 2019 — that time of year when the students and teaching staff start feeling the sunny mood of summer approaching — my daughter came out with another phase of media bashing her family and her parents, this time with the support of a prominent website that carried more national appeal than our local *Gazette*. Her article's title was pure, libelous click-bait: "My Family Was On A TLC Reality Show. Here's

The Dark Secret That Never Aired." It was as if time had been frozen in 2014. Would this ever go away?

No, social smears don't go away. But you have every right to overcome them.

This wasn't an all-consuming and destructive personal trial for me any longer. Time hadn't stood still since the original social smear, not for me, anyway. I'm back to writing and developing my debate materials business, this time with an online membership that makes it easier to run alongside my teaching. In fact, the two complement each other, with each informing and feeding the other. Wendy is talking about doing some writing of her own, perhaps finishing her third cookbook, a delicious tome she started before our smearing drama began. Half of my children are now grown, making their individual marks on the world, leaving Wendy and I "only" six minor children. Of those who have flown the nest, several own businesses, one is a videographer, another a poet who aspires to be a lawyer. They each have their own reputations to be concerned about. Weddings are popping up all around us. And I'm looking forward to when the next Jeub kid announces another grandchild in the wings. Our count — so far — is at eleven grandchildren.

Our family came together the Sunday after my daughter's article — spouses, fiancés, grandchildren included — and we discussed the frustration of the smear that seemed to never die. At the time we were nearly five years into this sad family drama, and we all knew that even if the offending daughter refused future calls from the media, someone, somewhere, would find old posts and whip up new chaos for us. It is now a never-ending reality of the Jeub family, a reality that none of us enjoy and no one wants. It is most frustrating to have your identity be hijacked at the whim of one girl. One daughter whom we all love so much more than she knows right now.

Together we resolved to create this book. My administration wished me well as I dedicated my summer — my first "summer off" as a teacher — to writing it. I set up a small Patreon campaign to include others who had experienced the pain of social smearing, and they walked with me as I told my story in raw, unedited fashion. My children helped me pull the story together, too, reading the bits and pieces to them that were so much a part of their lives, tragic as it was, but freeing, too.

And just as they helped me tell this tale, my family is helping me bring it to an end. We've been through quite a journey together through this dark and desolate land of social smearing, and I am very proud of how we have all landed. Today we are rebuilding our lives and reputations; restoring our love for each other and for life itself. But ending the book here would be incomplete without pulling back the curtain of my life just a little bit more; revealing a truth that, frankly, I'm not so proud of. And after that, stay with me for just a little while longer as my story of suffering turns into a story of solution, a most necessary final resolution to my family's epic journey.

"We've been through quite a journey together through this dark and desolate land of social smearing, and I am very proud of how we have all landed."

(Photo taken September 2020)

Chapter 9: Silence

My social smear reappeared right at the time I was supposed to overcome my family dilemma and return to my lifelong joy of teaching. That's when the social shamers seeped out of the ground and attempted to drag me down under again. How easy it was to have the old news of a social smear, long since forgotten, whipped up again into a frothing mess. To think that I was nearly removed as an English teacher for crimes I never committed, that I was never legally tried, and that I was never duly convicted. I was merely accused with unadulterated gossip, but instead of a healthy culture that resists and discredits gossip, we have a "cancel" culture with worldwide platforms that "repost," "like," and "share" the *hate*. I shudder to think of the potential power this new world has over us all.

I want nothing more than to slay the dragon of social smearing. My heart bleeds all over its trail, a trail already painted with the blood of my wife, my children, my children's spouses and their children, my extended family and friends. They did not ask to be known as fellow victims with a smeared public figure, and the weight of shame should not be theirs to bear. Six years ago when the smear initially splattered the walls of the internet, my business and its audience of speakers and debaters — moms and dads, too, who wanted the chance to peer into the life of a joyous family — felt the burdening shame. The thousands of students who read my textbooks, the teachers who bought my resources and the parents who sought more *Love in the House* from Chris and Wendy Jeub certainly felt associated with the kindred shame that fell upon the Jeub name.

My family's story is phenomenal in many ways, but I can't shake the question from my mind: Why? Specifically, why does the mob continue? Why *insist* on *hating?* I find the thought of *hating* others to be exhausting. You have likely asked the same, especially when you first laid eyes on the destructive post from a confidant or loved one. Your heart sank and you were embarrassed by the accusations — true or not — and you wondered, "Why are they doing this to me?" The inquiry echoes through our caves, but the beast remains silent and will not give an answer.

I believe I have that answer, and it was actually answered for me years ago, shortly *before* my smear tried to smother me. I find myself surprised I hadn't already woven it into my summer's work, for it holds so much power. But I now know that my fear held even more power over me. I admit I was afraid to be totally transparent, hesitant to share with you ... my *own* participation in the online mob. This fear is different from the revelation of libelous accusations that still remain filed away in the dark corners of the World Wide Web. My defense of this is today rather easy: I am not an abuser and can bravely stand against this false narrative. Vindication is behind me, but *redemption* still lingers ungranted.

I hope throughout my story you have empathized with my trials — perhaps you have even identified with them, being a victim of social smearing yourself. More and more of us are suffering from this shame. I find it most helpful to hear from others who have withstood the myriad ways the mob attempts to shame them — blog posts, social media, whatever latest web-induced method of torture that can be inflicted upon the innocent. The machine of social smearing is constantly changing. But I feel a genuine shame that is unique from the standard victim.

For you see, the leaders of the online mob were my students. I was their teacher.

This is not a metaphor; they were quite literally my pupils. And I taught them how to be keyboard assassins, tear apart the reputations of good people and ruin the lives of the innocent.

When writing I give little room for *hate*. I love to write about deep topics, and sometimes they can be controversial. Some of my favorite articles have been the most challenging, my hands shaking as I press "send" or "publish." I'm usually not regretful because I spend copious time researching, editing and rewriting the myriad details of my thoughts. I give myself ample time to consider all sides of an issue, looking deeply into the thoughts and ideas of those who oppose my ideas, those who have been cordial yet challenging, convicting but not condemning. I believe all authors of substance worth sharing operate from this perspective. This goes for any number of spokespeople well worth listening to — leaders, CEOs and presidents, pastors, teachers, etc. In a real way, they operate from a perspective of *love* rather than *hate*, communicating their passions, their fears, their desires to an audience they care deeply for, communities of people whom they love.

Today there is this counterweight: *the mob*. Their online attacks attempt to silence those whom they *hate*. You, too, have seen the responsive *hate* in online controversy. Take a moment and review some of the articles you have read online lately, especially the more interesting ones. Read the comments written below the authors' text. We have entire movements whose primary weapon is online smearing, and even automated "bots" — sometimes even from foreign governments out to stir dissension — all devoted to the sole purpose of smearing people and their ideas. Today it's practically old news already: even tech giants are muddying the water with shadow banning, comment ghosting and algorithms programmed to block content for the sake of promoting a social agenda and shaming the opposition into silence.

I communed with a developing "mob" that sprouted in the debate community, particularly homeschool debaters. They credited themselves as "recovering" from their Christian upbringings. These were a natural spring of homeschool kids — now adults — who were vocally challenging the leadership of old. Some in the mainstream media were picking up on their anger and disillusion, a popular magazine article dubbing the group "Homeschool Apostates," and showing how these young adults were exposing "hidden dysfunction" in the community of home educators. They quoted so-called victims of abusive homes, consistently making the link to the idea that homeschooling itself abided and covered up such abuse. There was always the implied connection, fallacious as it was, to a political goal of restricting freedoms and silencing those they hated.

This community grew and got organized. They launched a website where they published testimonials from other adults who reported abuses in their upbringing. The editors of the blog took aim at prominent educational leaders, especially the most religious ones, and extrapolated stories and expositions of their most radical ideas and beliefs. The writing style of this community was more impressive than your average keyboard warrior; these students were logical, complex and persuasive. They spread their rebuttals through social media and were bold challengers of Christian beliefs, focused primarily on teaching young adults to doubt the world in which they were raised.

I held out hope for these "apostates," like any teacher would hold onto hope for rebellious students. I had to. For some of these articulate, well-spoken, persuasive debaters were trained to be so in my own debate club. The founding member was an assistant coach at one of my debate camps years prior. They were now grown up and utilizing the techniques I had taught through my clubs, camps and curriculum. They used these skills to shame and condemn homeschool leaders, often their own parents. These young adults saw themselves as "liberators" of enslaved children trapped in hierarchical upbringings, sharing horrifying stories of abuse and neglect, vociferously shaming their parents and any of their sympathizers. They used their blogging platform to supposedly "expose the truth" and bring light to the embarrassing corners of the homeschooling movement. And they had the political aim to cripple hard-fought laws that protected parental rights to home educate.

At first I tried to understand them. I was even intrigued by the boldness of their writing. I reached out to their leadership and formed online friendships, eager to learn of their impassioned goals and aspirations. They insisted that they merely wanted to expose abuse, that they felt more empowered by online smearing than more proper channels of direct confrontation or the court of law. Shortly before my daughter went public with her rendition of abuse in our family's homeschool, I made a public declaration in a blog post of my own encouraging them as "change agents" and "freedom fighters." I attempted to encourage other homeschool leaders to be open to their message — presenting it as challenging and convicting, similar to much of my writing — and probing the idea that perhaps there was some truth to their brazen way of communicating. In my mind at the time, I was encouraging the homeschool movement to "lean in" and learn.

I was naive. You know the story of my daughters, two of whom had just finished a successful stint of debating and had an impressive display of trophies to show for it. They became friends with this community of disgruntled homeschoolers. They were soon coached to turn against their family, even to the point of fabricating a brutal narrative, from which the network of young adults ran roughshod through the internet with their exposé. My family has been trudging through the lies ever since.

When my daughter's initial blog post dropped on October 4, 2014, I not only reached out to her and her corroborating sisters, I reached out to the leaders of this online group, my former students. I wrote to them asking them to please get involved and help me speak sense to my daughters. My letter was desperate, and I hoped for sympathy. Instead, their response was cold and obtuse, calling my request "entirely inappropriate" and "manipulative and damaging." They took down my contributions from their site and replaced them with disclaimers of how I now was "discovered" to be "yet another abuser." Their full focus was to now retweet, repost and share the attacks against me and my family.

I lost so much hope that day, for my daughters as well as my students. It was a devastating blow that crushed my heart, my soul and even my physical body. I was a father and educator, hoping for great accomplishments from my children and students. These young adults should have been doing great things with their learned skills, but were instead serving as advocates for my ruin, standing firmly on the blogging platforms that I helped them create and promote, writing a deceptive yet persuasive narrative that I was a monster who wreaked havoc on the lives of the innocent, on my own children. And they were simultaneously doing this to a number of other families, always ready to serve up a political statement against homeschooling.

My deepest fear is that *I created the mob.* Like Frankenstein, I gave life to the Monster that now raised hell throughout the countryside of the internet. And like the creator of Mary Shelley's beast who hid in a cave-like dwelling when he fled his creation, so I hid in my shame and my fear. Perhaps my failing business and my troubled home life was because of the beast of social smearing, but it was a beast that *I* helped bring to life. Perhaps the past several years of rebuilding my family name and online reputation, claiming how unfair my online smear was, was a form of self-centered self-sabotage, a way for me to escape the brutally honest realization that *I helped create the mob*. Shelley's classic tale goes in the most terrifying direction: the Monster hunts down Dr. Frankenstein and murders his family. How similar had my story become? This experience was so traumatic, so inescapable, that I literally tremble at the thought of the mob returning one last time to ultimately destroy me — or worse, my family.

Am I blaming myself too much? I didn't pull the trigger on the gun, and I don't make up lies to shame anyone. As I mentioned, I love to write challenging works, but I refuse to condemn those who refute what I write. The mob claims I am an abusive father, but I stand firmly against the claim. Yet the shame of the accusation still hums along, the killer bats still swarm within its cave, and voluntarily opening myself up to more lies does seem irrational. Several friends have asked me why I'm so bothered by my online reputation, and if I am disturbed, why kick the hornet's nest? To mix classic tales, Dracula lies within, so perhaps I should leave the cave, never return, and get on with my life. To most this seems like the only sane move.

If you are dealing with a social smear, you likely want nothing more in the world than to return to your previously peaceful, tranquil life. Wouldn't that be nice? But that is ignoring the mountain that needs to be moved. You and I need to bravely face our fear, walk into the metaphorical cave, and confront our Monster.

This book is me entering the cave of my deepest admissions, a confession to the world, a cross-carrying surrender of my own sins and weaknesses. Would it be the end of my family and its name if I were to explore the truth embedded in the online fabrications against me? I fear this, but I fear more the legion of liars who may eventually hunt me down and ultimately win. It isn't enough for me to ignore the mob. There is only one way to subdue the swarm of bloodsucking Chiroptera: enter the cave and drive a stake into the heart of the lies.

I have been accused of crimes, you know that much. But I have much to share about the accusations. Set aside the social smear articulated by my blogging daughter, and I have a lot to say about how my children were raised, the mistakes I made as a parent, right along with the healthy changes Wendy and I have made. My estranged daughters do not know these truths, but they could if they would set aside the hate their mob so encourages. I also have much to share about religious "fundamentalism," the unearthed fear from the parental "bond of three" who used social smearing as an attempt to strip me of my teaching position. I would love to sit down with these parents and explore the harms of legalism and spiritual abuse. I have experienced similar pain, so painful that I have resisted much of it in my writings. I'd wager that we have much in common — my accusers and I — and open, intimate dialogue would lead to great healing, restoration and redemption.

I consider this to be the biggest loss in social smearing: relationships that never reconcile and never grow or change. My first year of teaching could have been so much better if I had been treated fairly, honestly, as a human being deserving of dignity and respect. I could have gotten to know people where they were, and we likely would have become friends. This is true for any estrangement, isn't it? A falling out with a neighbor, relative or loved one puts a huge downer on life. We alienate one another with hate, and social smearing added onto that hate makes it seem impossible to ever get along, let alone love again. What happens when I reach out in love and try to connect with those who hate me? In the social smearing world, I'm exchanging pearls for a hand grenade. And the haters have free and easy social media tools that serve to pull the pin.

Again, I ask the question, *Why?* I think I know the answer: *to silence.* As a writer I hate to admit it, but for the past six years my adversaries have succeeded. Wendy and I both stopped writing about our parenting — we even took down our family's website — and posting anything enlightening or challenging to the online world has been carefully, methodically calculated as a risk. Will it immediately make exactly the impact that we want? Because, our conviction goes, it will almost certainly be met with ridicule and hate. As already discussed, my ministry, business and teaching has been tempered and in some cases diminished to nothing. I walk on the most delicate eggshells, careful to avoid any topic worth exploring, fear of the mob rising up and suffocating me again. I have closed into a cocoon, silent on the issues that matter most to me, on topics that I feel I could help others with, about the love that I could share with the world. I've become an island; I've been *silenced.*

If you have a personal story with social smearing, you likely feel the same. If you've been attacked by an adult child as I have, you likely hesitate before sharing anything online about your family. Even at private gatherings, someone's innocent inquiry about how your family is doing leads to a struggle between being honest and being superficial. "Just fine" may be communicated, but your heart is retching in anguish, wondering how much the questioner really knows of your social smear. You stand accused, full of doubt, ashamed for that which you may not have even done. If your business has been attacked online — no matter how unfairly — you likely suffered a depressing bout of second-guessing the work you do for others. If you're a professional — perhaps a teacher like me — and the clients or employees or students you care most for turn on you and shame you online, you feel like quitting. Perhaps you already have. I don't blame you. Trust me, I've walked in your shoes, and I know the depth of your feelings.

The purpose of the mob is to *silence,* but my purpose — Chris Jeub's purpose in his writing, parenting and teaching — is the exact opposite. In my home, "shut up" is akin to a swear word, never uttered by Wendy or me and always rebuked when voiced by one of our children. *Silence* is the antithesis of the training I gave my students, the debaters who assailed me into silence six years ago. They took their training to a dark side that I *never* advocated. All the noble traits of debate — research, logic and reasoning, argumentation, rhetoric, understanding of opposing views and deep analysis — are to be used to promote discourse and dialogue. It is a communications pedagogy, not a technique to mute your opposition. Policy debates should lead to better laws, value debates should clarify complexities in conflicting situations, and factual debates should separate truth from fiction. My students — my daughters included — took these powerful tools and used them to silence those of us who promote good policies, wholesome values, and even facts and truths worth sharing.

I often explain to people that debating is not *fighting*, though I am starting to see the value of fighting a good fight. Done correctly, *fighting* builds up good policies, values and thoughts, as opposed to destroying them. Competition in ideas is always good for it sharpens the message and leads to truth. Some seem to think resisting argumentation is somehow peaceful, but I have found that such advocates often have their own hidden agendas and are merely waiting for an opportune moment to attack you as a person, to silence you as the opposition. It is *ad hominem* — Latin for "to the man" — and it is one of the most common logical fallacies implemented by the mob. I train debaters to be curious, not carnivorous, and to respect and explore their opponents' viewpoints and opinions. Debating is, to me, a most spiritual practice, "training the mind for action" (1 Peter 1:13), an act of "wrestling" with the angels (Hosea 12:4). Arguing is good; it is exercising the muscles of the mind, honoring and exploring the opposition and engaging in the outcomes in unison with so-called enemies. God himself calls us to do so, saying, "Come, let us reason together" (Isaiah 1:18). In fact, "love your enemies" (Matthew 5:44) is most evident in a fair and wholesome debate. If practiced, no matter where someone falls on the side of a political, moral or factual proposition, you and I can be most confident that the decision in the end will be much stronger than when initially proposed, and healing and restoration will result. Even between adversaries, argumentation and debate can bring redemption.

The socially smeared are truly *facing hate*, and the mob is the opposition, the enemy. *They are trying to silence you*. But you have a calling and a message that you were born to share, and you need to press forward and share it! The mob wants you to "shut up," to run away or curl up into a fetal position and lie on the floor, alone and ashamed. No! Whatever the attack that comes at you from the hateful mob, you must, with love, debate that attack! "Fight the good fight," Paul encouraged his pupil in 1 Timothy 6:12. "Take hold of the eternal life to which you were called."

So, why must the mob continue? Why do they *insist* on *hating?* Because they want to *shut you up*, that's why, but you need to fight back. Refuse to be silenced. *Face the hate*. Have full confidence that your "shield of faith" will protect you from the fire of the dragon until you can stand up and fight back.

Your next question is, *How?* I will explore that answer next.

My debate camps enthusiastically "trained minds for action" (1 Peter 1:13), but that training eventually turned on me as my ministry was essentially "canceled."

(Photo of Training Minds Camp, Estes Park, 2010)

Chapter 10: How to Think

This may just be the most painful yet most profitable journey of my life. Overcoming a social smear is a mountain to move, a volcano that seems to be erupting over and over again throughout our world today. This memoir is meant to vindicate me, absolutely, but the teacher in me won't allow for mere self-reflection. There has to be a larger picture, an others-focused side to all of this. So I'm laying bare my soul for the many more — you, perhaps — who have suffered similar pain, the many others who will in the future certainly fall victim to the riots of social smearing. To be totally honest, more than once I considered spiking this story altogether. After all, don't I have my reputation to uphold? I'm currently a respected charter school teacher with a publishing company on the side; both are essential parts of paying the Jeub bills. Wendy and I have wonderful relationships with our children — half now adults and many of them happily married — and we can't get enough of our growing brood of grandbabies (our 11th due soon). We have our daily struggles, but nothing close to the earthshaking public shaming that we have already withstood. Why kick the hornet's nest? Perhaps silence is the better, more civil option.

Jesus himself was famously silent when he faced Pilate in the days leading up to his crucifixion, but it would do us all well to remember that he had already said all that needed to be said. Today I am convinced that *not* printing these words, this story, would be surrender to the mob of hate, standing down to their intimidation and shame-based lies, never bringing resolution to this sad story. There is a fight to be had, you and I, with the rogue keyboard assassins who stand always at the ready, posting unfounded claims about us online. The mob is our common enemy, our new normal. They may be as close to you as a daughter, or perhaps a relative, coworker, neighbor, a mentor — perhaps even a stranger. And I'll bet that their accusations are not *totally* false, just truthful enough to intimidate you into a silent shell. Whatever is posted — no matter how untrue or fallacious — the internet is "forever," so the online claims will simmer to the top again, usually at the worst of times. You know this will happen — eventually. And the mob *knows* you know.

Though this may be our "new normal," we can exercise more control over its narrative than we think at first. There will be those around you who appear unsupportive, who doubt your reactions, and perhaps even sympathize with your smearers. Don't give them the power to write your story, to define who you are, or to manipulate your reputation or character. It's easy to get angry, to see them as spineless, perhaps as Judas priests willing to trade the good fight for a pocket of comfort. Hold judgment for a moment to give a curious look at the heart of their actions: *fear.*

Fear is the chemical weapon of the mob, and social smearing is its bombshell. Many of us respond in fear, rendering us inactive, burying the good that we have to share and instead pushing us into dysfunctional corners of shame. The mob relishes this fear in you, turning the dagger to accelerate the pain. It is the technique of dastardly dictators, of the most torturous interrogators. The mob's weapon of choice is used with extreme prejudice on those they judge deserving, and we think we have no other choice but to submit and be "cancelled." In today's media world, our fear allows the mob's hatred to win. Those of us who attempt to champion love in the world lay victim under its onslaught. As much as I would hope to think social smearing is a "paper dragon" — a weak and petty attempt to silence good people like me and my family — the dragon so very often wins the day. And love ultimately loses.

This issue of fear is familiar to me. Wendy and my story of bringing more-than-usual children into this world and our life had its moments of trepidation. We wrote about this in one of our earlier books *Love Another Child:*

> Imagine "fear" as an animal. It is a snake. Its sole purpose is to creep into your life and cripple you. While you may desire to have faith that moves mountains, Fear reminds you of the realities, the crumbling world out there, the uncertainty of chance, and especially your personal shortcomings. Anything it takes for you to refuse God's calling, Fear will use. Fear lies; it is its nature. When people turn their hearts from faith, Fear fills the leadership role, and it cradles those it deceives.

Do you see how fear works? When facing hate — pure, unbridled, unpredictable hate that rumbles through social media and online road rage — we think cowering will turn the blow of the abuser. But facing hate with fear never works. Cancelling my story — *any* story — for fear of another blow from the online mob is *giving in* and allowing the abuse to continue. Cancel culture is a culture of abuse, of compromise, of justification for abuse, of abiding in the continuation of abuse.

In light of my greater story, isn't this ironic? I've been accused publicly of heinous abuse, yet here I am the target of a cultural hammer of abuse called social smearing. Perhaps standing down would buy me some time. My family may make it a few more years before another gossip magazine decides to create more clickbait articles; I may make it through another year of teaching before a rogue parent digs up the same ol' story; I may be able to post a pithy article or two before the online mob whips up another campaign to *cancel* Chris Jeub. Is there any other escape from the humiliating blows other than standing up and fighting back at its insane rage?

I know this: Letting my story slide would not be safe, it would be surrender. There is a fight to be had, and it is a novel fight that doesn't fit nicely or neatly into a rational and sane world of dialogue and discussion. The mob is mad. Standing up for our reputations online does not resemble a debate round. (How I wish it did!) It is more like a hostage situation, the mob holding its victim in one hand and the pin of a grenade in the other; dredging up yet another smear to blow up our lives. An appeal to sympathy doesn't matter to the mad mob, and neither does the truth. Its cultish members are willing and empowered to reign down their hatred and ruin us. We must stand against them.

But *how? I will ask yet again.*

This new modern phenomenon is constantly changing, which means the answer to my impassioned question must also constantly change. Indeed, how we are to respond is a lifelong study. But against that formidable backdrop I will offer up some unique ideas that have grown from my epic trial. And you won't be surprised at this point to learn that they also stem from my background in academic debate.

What is debate? I define it as knowing how to "think, speak and persuade." I coach champions on how to win with these three steps, and I constantly remind them to do so *in that order*. Think first — know how to think properly before opening your mouth to speak. You will never truly persuade anyone until you are of sound thinking yourself. It is a pedagogy reflective of Jesus' admonition to "take the plank out of your own eye" before condemning your brother for having a speck in his (Matthew 7:3-5). Those who speak before thinking are loudmouths, and such fools do very little persuading. Thorough analysis with a great amount of patience is required before speaking out online. I look forward to the day when the mob submits to this thinking, but I'm not holding my breath. Even so, the smeared can use it just the same. Would you refrain from throwing a life ring to a drowning man just because you thought the rope might be too short? Sound thinking through the online madness is desperately needed.

In dealing with my social smear, I needed to be grounded in my thinking more so than I ever was required to be as a debate coach. When the mob is waiting on your doorstep ready to pounce on you for the slightest error, you need to become mentally razor sharp. Those near-perfect words I spoke to my daughters, turning the students of my slandering parents to my side, and positioning the local reporter to make me look like a martyr of faith, these were much more than just *words*. They reflected foundational *thoughts* and *ideas*, principles that shaped a proper and persuasive response, helping my cause and my family deal with the injustice of our smear. This *thinking* helped turn my trauma to triumph.

If you find yourself facing the hateful online mob aiming to destroy your online reputation, you will need to first know *how to think*. Virtually all of my debate courses begin with some sort of quick lesson in *logic*. I explain that logic is "the mathematics of thinking." The logical syllogism looks like an equation: *major premise + minor premise = conclusion*. Logic is the basis for all thinking, the "logos" of the beginning of the universe, even translated as "the word" in John 1:1, which reads, "In the beginning was the *logos*." Why basic logic classes have been largely removed from schools is a wonder. It reminds me of an early chapter from C.S. Lewis' *The Lion, the Witch and the Wardrobe:* "'Logic!' said the Professor half to himself. 'Why don't they teach logic at these schools?'" And that question is even more relevant to this century's educators than it was in the last.

Logic itself can be a complicated subject, but most of us find it easier to recognize the *failure* to think, and we see it on full display in social media, especially with the mob. We categorize these failures "logical fallacies." When you train your thinking to recognize logical fallacies, reading your social media feeds can be — at least on an academic level — interesting. Short answers are given for every little debate in the feed, so it is relatively easy to recognize and point out fallacies in thinking. I have found that people who are untrained in the *failure* of logic are prone to using them in their discussions. They usually grow angry with you for pointing out the fallacies, too, which is too bad. They should instead stop thinking fallaciously. But, alas!

As it is with currency, there is one truth, but multiple counterfeits. Logicians have explained hundreds of fallacies, and the study of these fallacies is incredibly rewarding as it helps you think correctly. When the brutal attacks came at me online, I can honestly say that I probably avoided a mental breakdown because I held onto logic (the Word!) during the years of smearing. Social smearing is devastating, but like strapping on steel armor, the bullets of attacks would bounce off when I cognitively recognized their fallaciousness. It's a superpower that debaters cultivate as they study logic and its many counterfeits, but it requires training — like a martial art — to recognize the fallacy, replace it with the truth and deflect the projectile-deception that was aimed to kill. Once trained in logic and its fallacies, the knowledge stays with you throughout life, perhaps becoming one of the most useful trainings a young person can go through.

In my experience with social smearing, I have found three fallacies that return over and over again. These were the fallacies that my daughters used against me, that the mob took up to fan the flames of trauma. I wrestled with the loss of my daughters and the humiliation of the smear, but I seldom surrendered to the "substance" of their attacks. Why? Because their words *weren't* the truth; they were fallacies. *Lies.* Let me explain these three fallacies that are consistently used in the world of social smearing. Knowing these — perhaps even studying them and memorizing them — will be like the Bracelets of Submission that keep Wonder Woman in her magnificent state of indestructibility. For you, they will help fend off incoming attacks from the mob.

1. Ad Hominem. Mentioned earlier, this is Latin for "on the man." This is the lowest of the low logical fallacy, the ultimate result being name calling and personal attacks. It is utilized to replace logic, to avoid the dilemma or problem altogether. Rather than thinking through the argument and engaging in a healthy dialogue of disagreement between two individuals, label your opponent a *jerk* (or *Nazi, racist, abuser,* whatever you want) in an attempt to shut down the debate. It sometimes works, but it shouldn't for those who understand logical fallacies.

> *Mob: You abuse your children!*
>
> *Me: There has never been proof of this, and only proof of its opposite.*
>
> *Mob: But you're a patriarchal fundamentalist, so of course you abuse your children.*

Whenever someone uses an *ad hominem*, you should realize you're dealing with the most elementary of thinkers, maybe even a *non-thinker*. You can chalk it up as a win without ever giving a response. In the world of debate, you have cornered your opponent and they have resulted to an illogical tantrum. You are now engaged in an argument with a child, and trying to reason with them at this level (saying, "I am not a patriarchal fundamentalist!") will go nowhere. This can be hard, especially when your name is being dragged through the online sewer, but debating with these people is folly. *Ad hominems* are childish and cruel, and people who use them should be called out as bullies, unfriended and banned from social groups. Others must do that for you, though. You'll get nowhere if you push back at them in the middle of your own mess.

2. Straw Man. This fallacy is a word picture: Envision an attack against a straw man instead of a real one, which is, of course, infinitely easier. You can stab away at that scarecrow all you want; it will not resist you. Here's how it works online: Your adversary paints a false picture of you or your argument, then proceeds to attack that falsity. Much like the *ad hominem* above, the mob often attempted to paint a picture of me that was easier to hate (calling me a "patriarchal fundamentalist," for instance). You will find that the haters online will virtually always *straw man* their opponent.

As an established writer and blogger, I had years and years of posts and books that the mob sifted through to find some sort of story they could *straw man*. I talked earlier about an article I wrote years prior to the initial smear that condemned a Denver pastor for arguing that girls should not be educated. When taking my teaching job, a parent took my condemnation out of context and built a straw man that looked like I was the one making this argument. Of course I didn't. She had thought that by building up a scarecrow Mr. Jeub she could shock other parents and even the greater community, and this was a major analysis of the article in *The Gazette*. I aptly defused the claim by pointing to its fallacy. From *The Gazette*: "'I have never advocated for an unequal education of boys and girls,' [Jeub] said, and he blogged against a pastor who 'believed such nonsense.'"

Simple, short corrections should be how you answer *straw man* fallacies. Do not attempt to defend yourself with long, lofty explanations. The mob is not interested in debating or exploring the deeper social ramifications of whatever straw man they're painting you as. They are attempting to ignore the argument, not engage it. Treat those who are prone to *straw manning* everything you say as you do those who resort to name-calling *ad hominems* — unfriend them. They aren't worth your time.

3. Appeals. There are several logical fallacies that attempt to "appeal" to something other than the logic of the conversation. These are the purpose of all logical fallacies: ignore the real conversation and focus on or "appeal" to something else. In an online thread with comments from many people, you will likely find appeals made by contributors who want to appear elevated above everyone else in the discussion for some reason other than the logic of the original claim. It is actually a sign of weakness, a psychological fear that some people tend to have within them, as if being wrong was a moral failure. So, instead of correcting their thinking, they *appeal* to some other entity to justify their wrongness.

Mob: I read online that you abused your children!

Me: You read it from gossip websites.

Mob: I have a degree in child psychology [an appeal to authority], so I can tell it's true.

Me: You don't know me or my children, so you have no authority to judge me.

Mob: Of course it's true! No one believes you [an appeal to popularity].

Me: No, it's not. Everyone who knows me personally has defended me.

Mob: They're probably just as ignorant as you [an appeal to probability and ignorance, as well as an ad hominem *attack against my friends].*

Me: You don't know my friends, either.

Mob: I'm being triggered by your arguments [an appeal to emotion]. Leave me alone!

Me: You attacked me. I'm merely defending myself.

Mob: You're a debate coach, just manipulating this debate [an appeal to motive, and ironically an appeal to my *authority].*

Me: You're right, I am a debate coach, but not an abuser.

Mob: You're sure abusing me! [An appeal to ridicule.]

These are all established *appeals* that people often make in social smears, as well as outside smears. I used to engage people online, and the exchange I crafted above is fairly representative of how I would debate. But as you can see, it too results in folly. This online mobster is clearly not going to deny her faulty premise (that of me being an abuser) and accept the honest truth that her conclusion is false.

All of these logical fallacies do the same thing: *avoid the truth by diverting the debate*. The *ad hominem*, the *straw man* and the numerous *appeals* to anything other than the truth are all meant to lead you off the trail of discovery and into worthless weeds of nonsense (which is the actual image of another fallacy, the "red herring"; a fake fish used to lead you away from the trail of truth). To some, remember, "the truth doesn't matter," and this defaults to the fallacious thinking you see in Facebook groups, viral Twitter tweets, and other social media debates. You can see why I consider most of the online "debates" to be no debate at all, and why I resist engaging them.

To be honest, I resist even offline debates with people who have little appreciation for the truth. Their consistent use of logical fallacies is a red flag I see early in any discussion that warns me of their shallow thinking. This may sound judgmental to call another's thinking "shallow," but it is accurate. Discussions with fallacious thinkers never get deeper than their personally held whims. You will seldom find these people conceding anything, changing their views or considering *your* point of view. In their minds, *their* truth is *the* truth. It's not. The truth is an objective reality and my beliefs must shift to adjust to that reality. When I meet someone who arrogantly thinks the opposite — that their subjective perception is the reality that everyone else should adjust to — I have learned that the best path is the path *around* them, not *through* them. In other words, avoid them.

But...! Mr. Jeub, you're telling me to never submit to the smear by never responding to the smear. Yes, I know this may seem like strange advice coming from a coach who trains champion debaters. And trust me, I feel the tug of temptation when I witness someone online or offline rattling off nonsense with justifications full of logical fallacies. Sometimes I do engage, but never for the purpose of persuading my apparent opponent. I will only engage when the opposition (the fallacious thinker) is *not* the person I'm trying to persuade, when an audience is watching the exchange and I want *them* to come to the truth. Debates are not exchanges between two people to persuade each other. This is a novice understanding of academic debate. Instead, a debate is an exchange between two people (or teams) to persuade an audience. Presidential candidates, for instance, aren't out to persuade their political opponent; they're out to persuade those watching. Likewise for any social media engagement, your posts should not be seen as your attempt to persuade the mob; they should be seen as persuading the many more observers who are weighing the ideas of the "debate."

Recall the online mob that came after me using the school's Facebook parent group. It was a mob of three, the most vocal and irrational contributors. Wendy and I were reading all of their posts while resisting the urge to heedlessly engage and defend our reputation. But we did post one very carefully worded response. We were laser-sharp in focusing on the observing audience, not the small mob. It was in response to several posts from the "bond of three" who were trolling through my online articles and, of course, the online gossip sites from four years prior. Wendy and I worked together in wording this — considering those online observers — and came up with the following. We decided Wendy should post it from her profile:

> *There is no abuse in our family and there never has been.*
>
> *We have graduated 3 of our children at [the charter school] ... We still have 5 of our youngest children going back next year. Chris has a business publishing curriculum. Last year he started subbing and he loved it so much he applied for a position. He has readjusted his busy schedule to go back in*

teaching full time. About 5 years ago some of our older children got involved in an online site that was full of fabrications. This site encouraged them to fabricate stories about homeschool leaders which my husband is one. All of it has been debunked.

Our family went through a devastating time when it happened but it is all pretty much reconciled now. The website has been defunct and the story about Chris was totally fake. When you apply for a teaching job there is a full background check done and fingerprinting and my husband has a squeaky clean record. FB and Gossip sites are not facts. Chris has a great public teaching record and your children will learn much from him.

That's the short of it.

Now, do you think we wrote this to try to persuade the smearing parents? This wasn't even a consideration. We were out to persuade the hundreds of other parents who may have been reading along, and this one response worked very well. Those parents were naturally concerned that the academy had made a mistake in hiring me, but Wendy brought a new perspective that online viewers may not have been considering. After making the clear and unapologetic denial of the accusation of abuse, she highlighted my strengths and our contributions to the school. She then gave the motherly touch of how difficult the original story had been on the family, but that it had been debunked. And Wendy's post — compared to the drawn-out sabre rattling of the "bond of three" that overwhelmed the Facebook group — was short, even ending on that note. Several observing parents confirmed later that Wendy's concise and focused response convinced them that the school had not made a mistake in hiring me. Some of them even became vocal advocates for keeping this reality TV "star" / debate coach on.

The concept of considering your audience has incredibly broad implications, more so than just debate or Facebook groups. This is a fundamental strategy that both ameteur and professional speakers apply; before all, consider your audience. All speeches should be built on this foundation. This makes you a better thinker, too, when asked to engage in simple conversations, even one-on-one discussions. Rather than placing yourself (your opinion, your ego, your ideas) at the center of your thinking, put the other's at the center. Your audience should always be at the forefront of your mind. This not only makes you a better thinker, it makes you a better person. Don't you appreciate people who do this with you, who have your ideas and interests and opinions at the front of their mind and the tip of their tongue? If you make a habit of considering your audience first, you will find yourself with more friends and more influence than you thought possible.

Friends and influence are invaluable when you later face the mob of hate in a social smear. This perspective is largely the reason why I did not engage in "debating" my daughters. The pull at my heart was to persuade them to come home, but I knew the stage of social media was not the place to do it. But friends did, and rightly so. When the mob attempted to hijack my Facebook profile, friends would come to my defense and keep me from being totally torn apart. They probably saw themselves as trying to persuade the mob, but I saw them as persuading those who were peeking in and considering the truth of the matter. This wasn't evident at the time, but later came to light when people would share that at first they thought there was truth in the original accusations, but after a while they saw how unbelievable it all was. They witnessed an online debate *about me*. If I had jumped in and berated my daughters for lying, my words would have persuaded no one, and the opposite effect would have emerged.

I hope this gives you more confidence, whether you're suffering at the hands of a social smearer yourself, or if you're helping a friend or family member who is. You've probably been in this position, wondering whether or not to engage by posting your thoughts in an online exchange — or even a face-to-face discussion at work or in a social setting. Should you stick up for the reputation of a friend? Or should you ignore the slight? I use this to weigh my decision: *Who is the audience?* If my audience is the person — one-on-one — and that person is known as a fallacious thinker with little care for truth, I will avoid the conversation (or take a radically different approach, which I'll explore in the next chapter). But if my audience consists of many more onlookers trying to sort out the online gossip from the truth, I will engage with the fallacious thinker. And, because I'm trained in logic and debate, I'll win. I may not convince my opponent of the truth, but I will convince the audience. That's called sticking up for a friend.

"Think, speak and persuade, *in that order*." And leave the heavy lifting to others, rather than trying to fight your way out by yourself. This is the only way to survive a social smear. If you find yourself in my shoes and are smeared by someone you love or appreciate, trust me, I totally understand your tendency to punch back and counterattack your accuser or the mob that follows along. My strong advice, though, is to resist defending yourself and let others come to your defense. Behind the scenes, you can even ask (beg) them to do so.

This doesn't leave you without personal options, however. Persuading the madness of the mob seems impossible, but it isn't. Traditional debate techniques work wonders when dealing with logical, reasonable people; dealing with *madness* takes higher-level strategy. Keep reading!

Training young people to "think, speak and persuade" is what my entire ministry was about. But they needed to do so IN THAT ORDER.

(Picture of students at one of my debate camps in Oklahoma.)

Chapter 11: Rules of Engagement

I remember the first time I thought I needed to get into Facebook. I attended an out-of-state debate tournament and stayed at the tournament director's house. She was communicating with all of her staff and students through Facebook — no phone messages or emails — and I witnessed how helpful the tool was. Both Wendy and I entered social media with a lot of enthusiasm, seeing it as a blessing and a boost in getting our greater message of *Love in the House* out to the world. My debate curriculum business, too, lassoed social media when it was growing in popularity. Added benefits included reconnecting with old friends, keeping in touch with relatives and posting the latest photos of whatever event my family had going on — which means posting something nearly *every* day! Add in the fact that Facebook was *free*, and I couldn't possibly have thought of a single thing that could go wrong!

Five years later our social smear hit. We faced the barrage of haters posting on our profile and pages, shocked by their vitriol and judgment. Wendy turned off all of her social media, but I kept it on. Cutting these virtual ties with family and friends was like trying to go cold turkey on a longstanding drug habit. Besides, I felt I needed to stay connected to social media's marketing benefits. I was the business owner and operator, *solopreneur* who took care of all things advertising and branding, so the last thing I needed was to drop the "free" social media arm of the good work we were doing as a family business. We had our books, our debate materials and even yearly summer camps for students. It's simple for you to go "off the grid," I told Wendy. But me? I saw that as impossible.

So I was plunged headfirst into the ever-deepening pool of online *un-*debate. This is not a world of controlled point-and-counterpoint. In competition, students do not need to overcome the preconceived biases of judges. Judges are trained educators who are prepared to set aside their own proclivities to rank the debaters fairly on the merits of their arguments and presentation. You can win a debate even if the judge is averse to your position. Not so with the online mob. With impunity they strike. You're a defenseless victim thrown among armed gladiators who relish the drawing of blood to gain approval from online spectators. It is ironic that Facebook uses the "thumbs up" icon to show approval, much like the ancient Romans showed approval for sparing the life of a stadium victim. We all know what "thumbs down" means, and though there is not this option in social media, a thumbs-up to a socially slanderous post does the same. And so these tech-savvy neo-Romans use their judgment to rip apart your reputation, your business or career, even your family. You're quite hopeless being thrown into such a lion's den. The mob is ready to tear you apart, and they seem to enjoy it.

I was not trained to face the giant of social smearing. My world of debate dealt with rational observers, objective judges and systematic argumentation that was academically measured and assessed. I am skilled at persuading the debate judge, but the mob? They are unreasonable and unmerciful. It is extremely risky to engage them, any chance for actual persuasion very slim. The mighty armor of logic and reasoning, which we so recently discussed, does virtually nothing to the internet beast. Principles and etiquette are beaten senseless. The giant needs to be taken down, but, sadly, it isn't going to be with traditional argumentation and debate.

There seems to be no way out. This is the haunting truth of so many of these sordid situations, and I would hate to end my book on such a negative note. Are we really stuck with social smearing as the upside-down world we all are intertwined with? I'm afraid so. We are all in this predicament, "facing hate" in the underworld around us. We may delude ourselves and think that we're into social media just to exchange photos with family members and have a little platform in a corner of the world from which to speak. If you've so far avoided the scary scrutiny of the online mob, let me tell you, your peaceful days are numbered. If you surf the waves of your social media feeds at all, you're cruisin' for a bruisin'. It's only a matter of time till you say the wrong thing, express the wrong opinion or share an unpopular belief. The unrelenting mob is ready to pounce and bully you into submission to whatever social conditioning they currently find acceptable. This is Orwell's world now, its goads tipped with a dystopian disease none of us anticipated.

This may sound like a downer — it *is* a downer! — but nothing is ever utterly hopeless. I've learned so much these last few years, and this book is my earnest attempt to share that which saved me from destruction. I leave four considerations for you, some that I have already suggested within the pages you have already read. These considerations are offered to help you wade through this brave new world of social smearing, and I believe fervently they will help you overcome the trials that lie ahead in *your* story.

1. Consider Advanced Persuasion

I have a bachelor's degree in English and an MBA, so I sat through my share of communications classes. These have helped in my professional life. Building credibility as a speaker, prodding a student through a difficult lesson, negotiating the investment and return of a contractual agreement, influencing others in meetings — all of these interactions require communication skills. But as I experienced social smearing, I began to wonder if any of the skills I'd learned actually did any good! The classes I took in college and my master's program seemed to share one fatal flaw: They assumed our audience was just as reasonable as you and I.

Such is not the case with your smearer, and especially the hateful mob that stands at the ready. They are not a paying audience ready to receive my prepared message, nor are they an eager student striving for a good grade in my class. In the world of business and even everyday interactions with friends and family, most of us rely on problem solving, basic instruction and just being *kind* communicators. Public smears of today are more like hostage situations where the terrorist cares nothing for you and makes unreasonable demands ... or else! How do you negotiate with people who live in this alternative reality?

This is where *advanced persuasion* comes in, and if you are *facing hate* of the mob — or, more importantly, from a family member you love or an associate you appreciate — advanced persuasion techniques will help immensely. I sometimes hesitate to talk too much about these techniques because they can sound manipulative when presented as the specific and detailed maneuvers in persuasion that they are. Some may accuse me of being intentionally conniving, of leading people down a dark path of deception. Quite the contrary, for two reasons. First, my attraction to *advanced persuasion* is a defense following the initial online attacks from the mob, who are the truly deceptive ones. Second, more importantly, my persuasive techniques are being used to lead people away from the deception that holds them so enslaved.

Remember my friend who suffered a divorce? He taught me strategies to help persuade my daughters to abandon their lies and desire their family once again. Remember the meeting I had with the couple from school who wanted me fired? There I practiced techniques that I had learned from my debate world of persuasion. Business and psychology are rich with negotiation strategies that work just as well in social media. And when smears come your way, you are able to tap into the "secrets to closing the sale" and be the "negotiation whisperer" that sways your opponent to your side. Simple understanding of some of these techniques can help immensely when dealing with social smearing.

We've already established that social smearing is like a hostage situation, which drew me to Chris Voss, an FBI hostage negotiator and author of *Never Split the Difference: Negotiating as if Your Life Depended on It*. He shares how negotiators will simply mirror the perpetrator's words, repeating his demands as a question, to show the criminal that you are somehow connected to his interests. Such a simple practice, but it works wonders when communicating with someone who is hostile. Remember when I saw my daughter at the Rush concert and wanted to persuade her to switch seats with my friend? "Come on, it's *Rush!*" I said, the exact same words she used with me when we first connected. Rather than rationally explaining my interests or trying to convince her to change hers, I mirrored her interests. This tactic works for FBI hostage negotiators, and it sure worked in my "hostage" situation.

So many of us approach social smearing with argumentation, trying to get those who hate us to change their minds and give us a "yes" confirmation. This is very difficult to do. Voss suggests that the last thing an anxious madman wants is to commit to anything, which "yes" does. Instead, revise questions to encourage "no" answers. Voss calls these "calibrated questions" that are measured to create the illusion of control, but actually draw out the conversation to help you better understand what your adversary wants. "Will you please stop this smearing?" is a lead-to-yes question, and a controlling hater will gladly reject you. Asking the same question in a lead-to-no way raises the probability of getting the answer you want: "Must you continue with this smearing?" The angry hater will be less prone to commit to "yes," and you may even get the "no" you want.

Voss goes on to encourage a more careful consideration of your foe's needs and desires, a strategy hostage negotiators call "tactical empathy." You want the social smearing to stop, but don't place that as your primary focus. Instead, seek out the smearer's real (often unstated) goal. Negotiations are more about information gathering than about winning a debate, and the information you gather will adjust your approach. Remember my daughter in Australia? Her sisters took some of what she shared about her stricter childhood to exaggerate the original online fabrication, and my regular tendency would have been to logically contest it. Instead, I "leaned in" and embraced her inner need for restoration and reconciliation related to past hurts from her childhood. This was not sappy or compromising. It was "tactical empathy," the most caring response that got exactly what both of us wanted in the end.

I know others who have suffered social smears like mine. Some have errantly held onto their traditional communication skills to attempt to persuade the hater in their life — adult or teenage child, angry spouse, extended relative, work associate or customer, etc. I have not seen much success in heated situations like these, and I have *never* seen argumentation and debate work with anyone from the crazed mob. These estrangements will be prolonged as long as you hold onto the methods that may work fine in the civilized and sane world but rarely if ever in the wide open wilderness that is social media. Move on to advanced persuasion and you may see some breakthroughs that will help restore your relationships and begin to rebuild your reputation.

2. Consider Engaging

The purpose of this book is to help you overcome social smearing. I hope I have convinced you that traditional engagement of the mob — online debates or counter-blogging — will produce very few victories, if any at all. Remember to consider your audience, and only engage in a debate when your audience is persuadable (and this is typically *not* your hater). There are much more successful strategies for the call of engagement. I identify with the conviction to engage online haters for ravaging your reputation, and sometimes the call is needed. Briefly return back to the prologue of this book. There I referenced real stories people have shared with me about their unique social smears — a neighbor spreading gossip, stepchildren labeling the stepparent "evil," a teacher facing irate parents, a father being ostracized from his son, a business owner smeared by a disgruntled customer. If you relate to any of these stories, I have suggestions for you to consider:

Gossipy neighbors. The strategies in this chapter will be most useful for you. In the example given, the neighbor complained online about the loud motorcycle driving at night, an obvious irritation to him. Mirror the cloaked complaint, "My motorcycle bothers you?" Apologize for this, but don't ask for permission, which would demand a "yes" answer. Instead, offer a solution, such as, "I will do everything possible to keep from firing up my motorcycle late at night from now on." Even if late nights weren't the original problem, what you're doing here is showing your neighbors that you care about them. In this case the neighbor posted his grievance on the community Facebook page, so if you engage with him through this forum, the entire neighborhood will witness your gracious response.

Stepchildren. The strategy of giving time — so hard to do when you're being smeared — is most successful when dealing with a situation like agitated stepchildren. Recall the straw man fallacy. The wife in this example is not "evil," but being accused of such has the potential to draw out your inner witch. It's not fair to judge good intentions in such a way, but the only path to overcoming the judgment is overwhelming kindness. "Show, don't tell" the saying goes, and give time for the truth of the straw man's opposite to be believed. Most helpful is the strategy of ignoring the offense. Trust me, I know how badly you want to rebut the accusation of being "evil," but pretend it never happened. Treat the stepchildren graciously and nicely, always showing the goodness in you. In time the truth will be self-evident … and freeing.

Irate parents. My heart goes out to the middle school teacher whose parents disparaged him online. I hope his administration was as supportive as mine! When being professionally attacked, the temptation will be to become defensive or counterattack. I fear these natural approaches only throw gasoline on the fire and lead to social media blowups that become embarrassing for the entire school or organization, not just you. I have found "extreme professionalism" to be a much better approach, which is what I clung to when the school's parents were blasting me online. Take the higher ground and fly straight as an arrow. On a deeper, more persuasive level, attempt to develop a relationship with the irate parents. If you can use advanced persuasion to get them on your side — or, at least, to significantly change the tune of what they've been posting online — they can become tremendous assets to your continued rapport as a teacher. A troubled-turned-supportive parent's attitude will trickle down to your problem student, and it will make teaching fun again.

Estranged children. The dad who shared about his son choosing a gay lifestyle is enmeshed in a story that is much in line with the story of this book. When your children lash out at you, your expectations for your growing family are crushed. Sometimes estrangement takes years to settle, so giving time is definitely warranted. Give your other children a chance to step in as well. At the time of writing this book, I have two estranged children — one still hostile, another docile but still separated — and I have chosen not to engage with them. However, my other children are free to engage all they want, and I have been very proud of how they have. Understanding that sibling bonds are arguably tighter than parent-child bonds helps shape up a proper perspective when dealing with estranged children. Parents seldom talk an estranged child out of hating them, but siblings have had great success. I have 14 children who love their parents and love the home they are in or return to as adults, and they all are hopeful that the two lost sheep will soften someday. I'm most hopeful for this, too.

Disgruntled customers. Understanding your audience is key when dealing with customers who are on a holy-terror crusade to ruin your business. In the case where an unwarranted negative review or social media post hangs out there — especially if your business depends on positive reviews — an answer is needed. In your answer, avoid arguing or correcting any assumption by the customer. In the case of the pregnant bride whose dress could not be altered anymore, the business owner should kindly apologize for her disappointment and remind the audience (who, by the time the tirage gets posted online, is *not* the disgruntled customer) of the money-back guarantee that was honored. The customer may not be right in her judgment, but business professionals always want their customers to win. Make sure your response reflects that. Most people nowadays expect some negative reviews, but your personal response of graciousness and professionalism — not argument or dissension — will persuade online review readers to do business with you.

These are all examples of how to effectively *engage* with the social smearer. Tread these waters carefully. If you find yourself defaulting to no engagement at all, that may actually be the safest reaction to social smearing. But, if you must engage, I urge you to utilize precise persuasion that will help sway the audience … not your adversary.

3. Consider the Cost of Social Media

Social media has much to offer, and it's *free.* Or is it? Businessmen recognize that nothing is really "free," that there are "opportunity costs" in anything that sells itself as free. Every minute you spend consuming is a minute lost creating, and wise businesspeople recognize that their resources should be spent on those things that create a better return. Sure, virtually all the social media platforms cost no money, but do they actually bring enough value to justify their use? We would be wise to consider the following costs of social media:

The cost of our time. The numbers keep changing (for the worse), but my latest fact check found that people spend an average of 2 hours and 22 minutes on social media per day. Even if you justified this time as "quality entertainment," this is a lot of time spent every day on entertainment, especially if you add in traditional entertainment like television and music. Consider the cost of your time that exceeds two hours per day. If the minimum wage is similar to Colorado's $12/hour, this amounts to a "free" service that costs you more than $10,000 per year. I used to feel that the cost of time was worth it for me, chalking it up as a business expense (since I connect with customers on social media), but 10 grand can buy me a pretty snazzy marketing package for my small business affairs. So I was wrong! The return on investment for me is *not* worth it.

The cost of our focus. Even when I don't have my phone out to thumb through feeds, I'm thinking about what I should next post. This takes a toll on us, more so than even time. My focus throughout my day should be on my wife, my children, my business and customers, the real experiences that I encounter. My phone in my pocket seems to call out to me for a new selfie, a clever quote or an opinion of importance to share with the online world. It is tantalizing to post something that is liked and shared, but that post expended a great amount of focus before I pressed "publish." I didn't realize the drain on my focus until I actually went on a personal social media fast. When your focus shifts from what the online world thinks to the real world in front of you throughout the day, you find your focus is on much greater matters. You might find that your own media fast reveals the same for you.

The cost of our freedom. For years the tech-world giants have been dubiously gathering private data, often without our permission, to harness its power and use it to market to us. At the time of this writing, the Federal

Trade Commission just fined Facebook $5 billion for illicit data harvesting, Google executives were caught on camera admitting to rigging search results that favored their political biases, and the United States Congress is proposing a bill to ban a feature of Snapchat for teenagers because of its manipulative nature. That's just this week in the news! This is beyond a social contract where we all surrender a few freedoms for some collective advantages in society. It is becoming clearer that "big tech" is pulling freedom out from under us, often without our permission or even knowledge.

These costs are high, and they should weigh heavily in your decision about how you interact with the internet and social media. If, heaven forbid, you are swept up in a social smear, the costs can bankrupt you. You can understand, then, the next consideration.

4. Consider Shutting It Down

There is something to be said about Wendy's strategy of going "off the grid." It *is* doable. In fact, it's perhaps easier than any of us want to admit. Before Wendy shut off all her social media when our social smear hit, she was the social media manager of our family business, but the trouble with social media are the thousands of strangers who demand answers and explanations. Demand *time*. So never mind them. If you weren't on her speed dial and weren't a *real* friend, there was no getting ahold of Wendy during the first year of our smear.

As I mentioned, I was not so willing to leave. I saw unplugging from social media equivalent to sticking your head in the sand, choosing to be oblivious to the world's events and volunteering for social obscurity. I think differently now. I appreciate social media for the connectivity it allows me, and I'm sure you do, too. But the elephant in the room — the evil dragon that is growing more sinister — is the online *hatred* that whips up so easily.

I did plunge my head into the sand a few times, shutting the social world down (or at least ignoring it) for the initial months of the smear, but I must admit that I kept "peeking under the hood." It was depressing, and it took its toll on me emotionally and mentally. It is dreadfully burdening to accept the reality that people genuinely *hate* you. I tried to read comments to understand the nature of their hatred, but it was an abyss of despair that left me deflated and demoralized. Online hate is the epitome of human depravity. You certainly see the worst of humanity when hanging out with the hate online.

As much as I love connecting with others, I cannot live in such an environment of hate. I have returned to social media, as has Wendy, but we now ration our intake. We no longer thumb through our Facebook feed to see what everyone else is up to, and I set up automations for my business to take care of most of my business posts. When the smear flared up again during my teaching employment, I went off the grid once more, totally shutting down my social media presence. I made this announcement to my Facebook friends:

> *I'm giving my full attention to my new English teaching job. Therefore, I'm unplugging from Facebook till October. Be good!*

I must be honest, those months were *so good for me*. The lingering need to post the latest tidbit of news in my family's life was gone. I was focused on my task of teaching, and I loved it so much that October came and went without a single fond thought for social media. I didn't return to Facebook till March. What once was a daily ritual of posting my latest adventure — and reading up on everyone else's — has since become perhaps a once-a-month chore. I feel that keeps me in touch enough, but I still sometimes think even that may be excessive. I hesitate to advise you to totally pull the plug. I would feel hypocritical to make such a suggestion. But, honestly, pulling the plug totally may be in my future. And I cannot envision missing it much.

Meals on our deck are filled with love and fun, evidence of genuine “love in the house.”

(Selfie taken in 2019)

Chapter 12: Love in the House

Wendy and I started a new tradition two years ago. It came about from the lack of connection, the inability to keep up with all the commotion of a maturing large family such as ours. The idea was to gather weekly at a time that worked best for all of us. That time turned out to be ... breakfast. Not everyone can make it every week, but when they do, it sure makes for a full house. If you drive by at that time, you'll see cars lined up our road as if we're having a church service. If the weather is nice, we'll have picnic tables stretching across our 20-foot-long front porch. We'll be enjoying eggs and bacon, toast, orange juice and coffee. We've talked about getting a restaurant-grade coffee maker, but for now our 12-cup pot is loaded several times through the morning to keep everyone buzzing. The conversations roll through the meal, ranging from important announcements of calendar items to whatever's new and hot that everyone should know about. Then we go our separate ways. Some go to their in-laws, some venture off on some adventure, others go to various jobs. These mornings have become true, restful blessings.

Thank you for joining me (and my family!) for breakfast, as it were, and walking with me through the story of my social smear. It means the world to me that people like you have listened to and learned from and accepted my attempt to vindicate my name. The Jeub family is the exact opposite of that which the mob has tried to portray us. I wish you could be a fly on our wall and witness the joys and struggles of our loving home. You'll become a bit jealous. I wouldn't dream of trying to fool you; we have our arguments and dysfunctions, but they are wrapped with love and respect for one another. We are not claiming perfection; nothing of the sort. Throw a hot political topic on the table during a robust breakfast and you'll see a House of Commons come alive. Ask me later about our aggressive, cutthroat, fight-to-the-finish games of Nerts. They are wild!

Yet when I meditate on how much of an influence social media became in my life even prior to my online attack and social smear, I am honestly surprised at how much it led me away from more important matters. Like a thief in the night, my time wisped away as I checked online feeds and considered my next post or comment or thread of debate. It isn't as if I had nothing to do. I have a large family, property to tend to, businesses to manage, students to teach. Does my precious phone take precedence over these things? Which is more real: the calling God has given me (family, career, etc.) or the artificial "likes" from an online world?

The drama of my smear involves many more than just me — it involves my family, of course, but also the speech and debate community that I publish to, the school that employs me, the students I teach along with their parents and siblings, the small town that I live in with my neighbors and friends, and my extended family near and abroad. I feel a patriotic responsibility, too, as an American, with a daughter and her family abroad, which burdens me even more with a worldwide concern for social smearing and the great damage it can do to others. I have plenty of friends, and many of them fear for me and the possible rising of the online mob that may come after me yet again. And maybe there's even a touch of fear in all of this for them, as well. Perhaps, they wonder, the mob might pull them in the next time around, inflicting shame on *their* families, *their* schools, *their* businesses and communities.

I recently sat across the table from a professional associate who flat-out told me that he wished I wouldn't publish this book. Like me he is a victim of social smearing, just a Google search away from all sorts of incriminating claims of impropriety and character flaws, primarily in his business dealings. No evidence, mind you, just claims — and those claims are out there as fodder for the mob. My friend saw this book as resurrecting the dragon of hatred back into his life. I explained what the last few chapters explained, that suppressing the message of my book would be surrender, that we should instead fortify ourselves and defend our reputations. But his eyes were still filled with genuine fear.

I have another friend who appealed to me through social media messages. He's a like-minded homeschool father of several children, his oldest daughter staging her own little social smearing campaign, not as brutal and public as mine, but just as painful. "You shouldn't write this book," he told me. "I think the world of your family and understand why you want to write this book. But this new writing project is probably not your best use of your creative resources if you really want to reconcile. … It just adds more drama and bitterness to the conflict." My friend sees my story manifest in his life, and he fears more separation from his own daughter because of my public pushback.

Of course, the mob did not want me to publish this book, either. As its first chapters were published, one of my daughter's most vocal advocates has been again trolling my social media, attempting to post inflammatory responses to my memoir about posting inflammatory responses. He sees himself as a protector of abused children, of which my daughter — in her and his alternative reality — is a victim. Again, claims with no evidence. He is not an eyewitness nor a confidant of our family, hardly even an internet "friend." He claims to be a liberator of tormented children, but he doesn't even understand the true underpinnings of social work. He has become, I guess, a "professional smearer," searching the internet from the comfort of his apartment to find embarrassing stories about families like mine. He claims that I'm causing more pain and destruction by voicing my rebuttal publicly. "You are throwing gasoline on a fire," he posted recently. "That's not how one should address abuse and trauma." This from a man who has become an expert at wielding a gasoline can … as long as it serves his own purposes.

Then, of course, there are my very own beloved children. I am blessed with 16, but even more richly blessed as we add spouses and grandchildren and in-laws and their extended families, multiplying our bounty to overflowing. My, how my life is full! But my heart still aches for the two currently estranged from the rest. At the time of this story's publication, these two adult children still hold onto the original fabricated story of abuse, and if they ever feel the desire to retract their story — perhaps pay us a visit, sit around our dinner table, and feast together with our growing brood — they have the world of haters to fess up to. I can imagine they feel a tremendous burden if they ever wanted to return home. They've created a false narrative of what goes on behind our front door, and that narrative was believed by countless internet followers who would not appreciate being played, and they will care nothing of any personal revelations my daughters may have. Hence, my daughters are trapped between the rock of this book and an internet mob, unable and unwilling to recant or retract.

You've read this book, so you know already where I've landed when it comes to indecision, fear, misgivings and, yes, even gasoline. But where are *you* on this path? Do you cower in fear for a past sin that might be exposed online? Do you have a social smearing child (or spouse, ex-lover, sibling, neighbor, student, coworker, customer, etc.) who tears you to pieces on social media? Is some of your life ruined by an online reputation you didn't deserve — or maybe you humbly accept you *did* deserve? Perhaps, on the flip side, you've publicly dished out some self-righteous dirt on others. Have you perhaps thought yourself a "social justice warrior," now coming to realize the error of your ways? Do you have some fessin' up to do, some posts to take down, some apologies to make? I've had hate in my heart before, and I've had to humbly apologize for faulty claims I've made — both online and off. This entire book may seem to condemn the "haters," but frankly, I've been in their shoes. We have all walked in them.

Every bone in my body resists conspiracy theories, but I'm quite certain that *we have all been played*. It doesn't matter your religion, politics, upbringing or education, we've all been suckered and manipulated. In today's internet world, unsuspecting foes find themselves roped up in a big-tech puppetshow, a drama that none of us signed up for and none of us anticipated. Who doesn't get wound up in a rage when they see a dogmatic post, a political meme, a blazing truth (or untruth) on their profile feed? Our internet world is — like it or not — calling us to action, to fight some sort of fight, to pit us against one another. We read our likeminded news sources and our preferred blogs, then whip up the hype by liking, sharing and commenting. Our judgment hammers down in our rioting corners of the internet, taking eye-for-eye and tooth-for-tooth, thinking all the while that we're bringing justice into the lives of others.

But in truth, we are merely caustic, cruel and jealously judgmental. In reality, we're being conditioned *to hate one another.*

I am not the only one speaking out about this deeply sinister side to social media, of which social smearing is just one of many weapons in its desolate wasteland. This book is deeply personal, a narrative of my struggle, and is therefore hardly an exhaustive critique of the greater problem we find ourselves in. The technology world has dubbed it the "social dilemma" created by informative and helpful internet tools that can do so much good in the world while simultaneously tearing us apart and pitting us against one another. If you haven't already, watch Netflix's most current hit, *The Social Dilemma,* a documentary about former big-tech developers who are now making a clarion call to regulate the very technologies they helped create. Its bottom line: *We're all being duped.*

I have come to a most significant point in my journey. I've woken up to the reality of how my online "face" has stolen the love from my life. I do my best to "face the hate," but the flesh in me wants to hate back and flagrantly condemn my attackers while fighting the holy war for my reputation. But I can only do so by "turning the other cheek" (Matthew 5:39), a higher calling to love and rebirth. So, instead, *I lean in.* I am selective with my online posts, currently just promoting this book project and announcing the biggest events of my family. I've become a tactical engager, opting for purpose and persuasion in my online friendships. Some people have expressed disappointment with my new habit of rationing social media, but I am like an addict who fears returning to the poison that once controlled me. My life of social sobriety is less intrusive, more purposeful and harnesses real life.

Are you feeling the same? Is this the beginning of a much-needed Great Awakening across the world? May it be so.

When Wendy and I wrote *Love in the House* — published about the same time we got into social media — we anticipated writing many more books in its wake. We could have, but I must admit we got swept up in the media flow of having to keep up with online expectations and pressures. Our purpose in life seemed to get hijacked as we tried to present ourselves online. We tried to be authentic, realistic and truthful, but the rat race stampeded us. Our purpose in life — God's calling — was swept aside.

The subtitle of that first book, "Filling Your Home With the Greatest Commandment," has now returned to its rightful status of full-blooded conviction in our family. That which takes from the love in our life must be rationed. If it is an addiction, it needs to be eradicated altogether lest it steal all the love we have left. Facing the hate of social smearing is a devastation I wish on no one, but it has caused me to pay attention, to sit up and take heed of the dangers that lie at the front door to my home. It seems as if the events of these past six years have laid before me a choice between a fake self and a real calling, a Facebook "family" and my flesh-and-blood Jeub family, an online jaunt and a heavenly purpose, even death and life itself. The artificial is tempting and fleeting in its rewards, but the real deal — the love of God and his greatest commandment to exemplify that love in my life — is returning front-and-center in the Jeub home.

I now stand renewed, rejuvenated, born again to a greater understanding of how love must prevail. The worm of hatred is no longer allowed to fester in my life. I may have been accused of heinous crimes, and my manufactured online narrative has attempted to enslave me to my guilt. It will not. I am both innocent and free. I patiently wait for my daughter-accusers to return to their welcoming home of love and prosperity, but that time is not for me to manipulate or judge.

As for me and my household, we will serve the Lord. His greatest commandment is to love him and others; this is our paramount burden in life, a great and glorious burden indeed. This is real life, and we aim to open that life up to as many as we possibly can.

Including you. May my story and the principles within this book be a blessing to you and your heavenly calling in life. When social smearing gets in the way, may you overcome this modern obstacle as you follow your heavenly call.

Our most recent family photo, December 2020.

Afterword, Early 2021

I put down my pen on this book months ago, but now — mere days before going to press — I marvel at the timeliness of this memoir. The world has changed dramatically. A pandemic has convinced governments to shut down entire economies. The election of an American president has been compromised, in one way or another. And tech companies are brazenly cancelling those who attempt to counter the politically correct view on the world's most important news. These unbelievable events are unfolding before us across our favorite media channels. Social smearing has taken center stage as political figures, companies and the media attempt to shame, belittle and silence the concerns of millions of people.

The world has radically changed, and it is disturbing.

Let me ask you a question: Why did you pick up this book? Think back to the initial thought or idea that drew you into my story. I doubt it was to make you laugh. Inspiration isn't it either, as there is little more bleak than social smearing. This is a memoir of tragedy, hardly light material. I'll bet you were looking for answers to this modern phenomenon. You are either socially smeared yourself, or you're concerned about the broader, global problem we face in our social media world. You are just as disturbed as I am. And I truly hope my story helps make better sense of it all for you.

But after that, if you're like me, you're asking yourself, "What can I do?"

Among others, the story you just finished proffers this practical answer: Explore the hidden truths of your smear, restore relationships with strategic persuasion and love, and rebuild your reputation with a firm grounding in the truth. Tough as it may seem, I believe you can weather your storm and come out stronger in the end, just as I have. Get back on track on your unique path in life, and if social smearing is the next mountain in your way, then *move it!* Embrace the strategies in this book and, with truth on your side, you will be victorious.

Let me tell you what I'm doing.

I'm doing the same thing I did when I initially responded to my social smear. Recall that at the beginning of the book, my life was rocked by online fabrications and lies about my family. If these attacks had come from strangers I would have responded with my expert tools of persuasion and launched a full-scale invasion into the online world of debate. I would have likely succeeded. But my fight came from within my own family, from precious children whom I love. So I chose instead to lean in and seek the answers I needed to help get me through my storm. I traveled across the country to connect with advocates and adversaries alike, even a trip around the globe to Australia. My social media presence fell flat as I withdrew from the noise and regained my footing in life.

Was I afraid? Of course I was. You know that. But I had few options other than scrounging up enough courage to embrace this new journey through my socially smeared life and seek the truth. As you and I now know (with 20/20 hindsight), my "withdrawal" had purpose and meaning to it. I retreated, retooled and regrouped my family, and eventually reentered life's great war of words and ideas that is my calling.

I'll admit, I live a complicated life — kids and grandkids, careers and businesses, etc. — and I enjoy the chaos of my supersized lifestyle. But I do sometimes wish I were more of a simpleton. Decisions would be much easier. As I witness the draining, divisive and deceiving tactics of social media and the so-called Big Tech companies, I once again feel the same draw to withdraw that I felt so many years ago. I'm retreating to find that cadence where I am in lockstep with God and His will in my life. I need simplification, a new routine or system, solid ground for which to plot my next plan. Just like you, I've got more questions than answers. I feel I'm venturing onto a new venture yet to be determined.

Today, two weeks before the first wave of this book hits the shelves, I pointed my own advice back at me … and cancelled my Facebook and Twitter accounts. This is definitely simpleton behavior for an author with a substantial following. I run the risk of losing paying customers in markets that could exponentially grow into lucrative and impactful opportunities. But these "tools of the trade" have led me off my path too many times now. I'm like an addict letting go of his addiction. Yes, I'm withdrawing, and I will certainly feel *withdrawals* in the coming weeks and months. But I'm in this race for the long haul, not temporary satisfaction. I seek truth, and I believe I will find it in the end.

I hope the same for you. We all have our battles and trials in this Brave New World, and I suspect our greatest and gravest are yet to come. While I hope you enjoyed the story of this book, I hope even more that it will accompany you on your own journey. Consider me a friend willing to help or listen, someone you can count on to encourage you through whatever God is calling you to do.

The Lord knows I seek the same kind of friendship in you.

One Final Thought

There is no better way to stay connected than directly through ChrisJeub.com. There on my personal website you will find my contact information, new blogs and resources, fun freebies and vibrant discussions. The best part? I have no fear of being deplatformed or socially smeared by any one of the Tech Titans. So join me today by checking out the site and subscribing!

Once there, please don't hesitate to reach out to me. A surefire way to grab my attention would be to start your story with this: "I just finished reading your book and …" That will be all it takes to start a deep and rewarding conversation!

Made in the USA
Middletown, DE
18 September 2022

10115051R00118